"JUST WAIT TILL YOU HAVE CHILDREN OF YOUR OWN!"

"JUST WAIT TILL YOU HAVE CHILDREN OF YOUR OWN!"

Erma Bombeck

With Illustrations by Bil Keane

Thorndike Press • Thorndike, Maine

Library of Congress Cataloging in Publication Data:

Bombeck, Erma.
   "Just wait till you have children of your own!"

   Large print ed.
   1. Large type books. I. Title.
   [PS3552.059J8 1984]   305.2'35'0207   84-8580
   ISBN 0-89621-552-0

Large Print edition available through arrangement with Double-
day & Company, Inc.

Cover design by David Freedman

To Thel Keane and Bill Bombeck,
without whose cooperation with the authors
the teenagers and consequently the book about
them could not have been produced

Dear Bil:

I hope you will understand why I cannot start the book today as promised. It was our original idea to write and to illustrate a volume on teen-agers that was not a put-down, but would be filled with love, humor and poignancy.

How does aggravation, hostility and pain grab you?

Some women are lucky, you know. They gave birth to babies. I gave birth to teen-agers. Our daughter was born with a Princess phone growing out of her ear. Our son was born with his foot extended in an accelerator position and a set of car keys in his little fist. The third was born hostile. (Even in the nursery he staged a protest to lower the age of birth to a five-month fetus.)

This morning was unbelievable.

"Mother, is that all the breakfast you're going to eat?"

"I'm not hungry."

"You say that now but later on you'll eat a lot of junk that will only give you acne. Here, at least eat a piece of toast."

"If I keep eating, I'll outgrow my new suit. And I want to look spiffy for Maxine Schmidlap's Tupperware party."

"You use that word a thousand times a day. Is that the only word you know?"

"I can't help it. It says what I want to say. By the way, I need the car today."

"You should get more exercise, but if you really need it, pick me up at school exactly at three. Oh, and do something about those white socks, Mom. They're absolutely orthopedic looking."

"All the other mothers wear them."

"But you're not everybody. You're my mother."

"You kids better hustle or you'll be late for school," I said.

"Have a good day," they chirped, "and remember you can't do housework and watch 'As the World Turns' at the same time. Get your dishes and laundry over with. Then you can watch TV."

When will they understand that I am grown up, Bil? When can I have a life of my own? When will they stop smothering me? Criticizing me? Spelling in front of me? I'm forty-three years old. I want to be treated as an adult.

Truly, I am sorry I cannot start a humorous book on teen-agers today, Bil. Maybe tomorrow . . . when I am not so g-r-o-s-s and my acne clears up.

Erma

1

How I discovered I was living with a teen-ager

Acute withdrawal

"I'll be in my room."

"Gosh, Mom, nobody's PERFECT!"

In my mind, I always dreamed of the day I would have teen-agers.

Young boys would pinch me in the swimming pool and exclaim, "Gee, ma'am, I'm sorry. I thought you were your sensuous daughter, Dale."

The entire family would gather around the piano and sing songs from the King Family album. And on Friday nights, we'd have a family council meeting to decide what flavor of ice cream their father, Ozzie, would bring home from the ice-cream parlor.

It never worked out that way. Our teen-agers withdrew to their bedrooms on their thirteenth birthday and didn't show themselves to us again until it was time to get married. If we spoke to them in public, they threatened to self-destruct within three minutes. And only once a young boy grinned at me, then apologized quickly with "Gee, sir, I'm sorry. I thought you were Eric Sevareid."

Heaven knows, we tried to make contact.

One day when I knew our son Hal was in his bedroom, I pounded on the door and demanded, "Open up! I know you are in there staring at your navel."

The door opened a crack and I charged into my son's bedroom shouting, "Look Hal, I'm your mother. I love you. So does your father. We care about you. We haven't seen you in months. All we get is a glimpse of the back of your head as you slam the door, and a blurred profile as the car whizzes by. We're supposed to be communicating. How do you think I feel when the TV set flashes on the message 'IT'S ELEVEN O'CLOCK. DO YOU KNOW WHERE YOUR CHILDREN ARE?' I can't even remember who they are."

"I'm not Hal," said the kid, peeling a banana. "I'm Henny. Hal isn't home from school yet."

Another time I thought I saw Hal race for the bathroom and bolt the door.

"I know this isn't the place to talk," I shouted through the keyhole, "but I thought you should know we're moving next week. I'm sliding the new address under the door and certainly hope you can join us. I wouldn't have brought it up, but I thought you'd become anxious if you came home and the refrigerator and the hot water were gone."

A note came slowly under the door. It read,

"I'll surely miss you. Yours very truly, Hartley."

Finally, my husband and I figured out the only way to see Hal was to watch him play football. As we shivered in the stands, our eyes eagerly searched the satin-covered backsides on the bench. Then, a pair of familiar shoulders turned and headed toward the showers.

"Hey, Hal," said his father, grabbing his arm. "Son of a gun. Remember me? I'm your Father."

"Father who?" asked the boy.

"You're looking great, Hal. I remember the last time I saw you. You were wearing that little suit with the duck on the pocket. Your mother tells me you're going to be joining us when we move."

"You have me confused, sir," said the boy. "I'm not Hal, I'm Harry."

"Aren't you the guy I saw poking around our refrigerator the other night? And didn't you go with us on our vacation last year?"

"No, sir, that was Harold. Incidentally, could you give me a lift to your house? I'm spending the night with Hal."

We thought we saw Hal a few times after that. Once when we were attending a movie and they announced a car bearing our license number that had left its parking lights on, a rather thin boy raced up the aisle, but we were never sure.

Another time at a Father-Son banquet, some-one noticed a resemblance between my hus-band and a boy who hung on the phone all night mumbling, "Aw c'mon, Wilma," but that was also indefinite.

One day in the mail I received a package of graduation pictures and a bill for $76. It was worth it. "Look, dear," I said to my hus-band, "it's Hal." Our eyes misted as we looked at the clear-skinned boy with the angular jaw and the sideburns that grew down to his jugular vein. It made spotting him at graduation a snap.

"Son of a gun," said his father, punching him on the arm, "if you aren't a chip off the old block, Henny."

"Hartley," I corrected.

"Harold," interjected another voice.

"I'm Hal," said the boy graduate, straighten-ing his shoulders and grimacing.

"Hal who?" we all asked in unison.

Sibling bill of rights

"Mom! It's lookin' at me again!"

"Notice anything different about my face?"
"Yeah. Your acne stands out more."

I know it is too late now, but I have long felt that I was foolish not to limit my family . . . to a parakeet with his tongue clipped.

That way, I would have escaped a confrontation with the Sibling Bill of Rights.

For years, I have deluded myself into believing I was raising children. Wrongo. I am not raising children at all, but cold, austere computers who are equipped with memory banks. When one child is fed a gift or a favor, the eyeballs of the other one roll around wildly. His entire body shakes, a buzzer sounds, two bells ring and a voice says mechanically, "They never bought me a watch until I could tell time."

What the memory bank lacks in logic, it makes up for in sheer volume.

One will say, "You got the biggest piece of pie for supper. That means I get to sit by the window the next time we go on vacation."

Or, "Richey's broken arm cost $55. Since I wasn't stupid enough to break my arm, can

21

I have the $55 for a car?"

Or, "I made the last tray of ice cubes. That means you have to pass ball with me the next time I ask you."

It is not important that they cannot remember where they left their Sunday shoes. What is important is that they have retained in their memory banks how much allowance they received in the third grade, what they got for their second birthday from Grandma Tibals, the exact hour they were put to bed when they were five and the precise moment they stopped getting those lousy home haircuts.

The memory banks go into full gear at bedtime.

Teen-ager: You little creep. You used half a can of deodorant. I wasn't even allowed to use deodorant until last year.

Little Brother: Can I help it if you're a late smeller?

Teen-ager: Keep it up. I'm going to tell Mom why she has ants in her registers. You think I don't see you kicking your crusts down there. When I was little I had to eat everything on my plate.

Little Brother: And I'll tell her how you stare at me at the table and say "eeeeeee" under your breath.

Teen-ager: You get away with murder. Just

because Mom and Dad had you late in life. (twenty-six!) Do you know how old I was before I got my first bicycle? I was five. You got one before your diaper dried out. And the bike I got didn't have five gears and a hand brake. I got one with the skinny tires and dumb-looking bell and we wore fat pants that always got caught in the chain. (Editor's Note: The more this story is told, the more primitive the vehicle becomes until he will eventually be driving a chariot in a loincloth.)

Little Brother: Big deal. I gotta do my homework.

Teen-ager: Wow. If that doesn't beat all. I didn't have homework until I was a freshman.

Finally, I could stand it no longer. "Boys!" I yelled, "I want you to run down to the shopping center and get some bird seed. Petie acts hungry."

I saw their eyeballs start to roll. Bodies began to shake as a buzzer and two bells began to sound. Finally, a voice said mechanically, "We never get to eat before we go to bed."

"It's simple," said the other voice, "Mom always liked the bird best."

Telephone fever

"Something wants to mutter to you."

"Kathy?"

The other night I nearly fell off my chair when a voice said, "MOM! TELEPHONE!"

I wandered through the house shouting, "Where! Where!"

"IN HERE!" shouted my daughter. "IN THE HALL CLOSET!"

I crawled in under a topcoat and felt my way along the cord to the phone.

"Are you going to talk long?" she asked.

"I don't even know who it is," I answered.

"I didn't ask who it was," she said, "I asked if you were going to talk a long time."

"I won't know until I know who it is," I said firmly. I grabbed the receiver and said, "Hello."

"Who is it?" she asked impatiently.

"An obscene phone caller," I whispered.

"Are you going to be long?" she persisted.

"I don't know," I said, listening intently.

In the small bit of light that was available, I saw my daughter dance up and down in front of me, grabbing her throat while her eyes bugged and her tongue began to swell.

"Pardon me, sir," I said to the caller. "Could you hang on just a minute? My daughter, Karen, is in front of me and is trying to tell me one of three things: (a) Her pantyhose are too tight and have cut off the blood supply to her kidneys, (b) she is thirsty and is asking permission to split a soft drink with her brother, or (c) she will die if she does not get the phone within the next minute and a half."

Covering the phone I said, "Karen, what do you want?"

"I have to call Celeste," she said. "It is a matter of life and death."

"In a minute," I said and returned to my caller.

The closet door opened and my son poked his head in and pantomimed, "Who is it?"

"It's an obscene phone call," I mouthed back. "What do you want?"

"Do you have a no. 2 tomato can? Fifteen jelly beans? Four buggy wheels? And a box of cocktail toothpicks?"

"Not on me," I said.

Another figure crawled into the closet. It was getting crowded. "Mom, who are you talking to?"

"An obscene phone caller."

"The dog wants out," he said. "What's obscene mean?"

"Get a dictionary."

"You want the dog to go on the dictionary?"

"I want you to look up obscene." Into the phone I said, "Really, I am too paying attention. It's just that . . ."

My daughter crawled in the closet with a poster that read, "FIVE MINUTES WILL BE TOO LATE."

My son persisted, "It can be a no. 2 can of orange juice if you don't have the tomatoes."

"PLEASE!" I said aloud.

Finally, my husband poked his nose in the closet.

"Is that Grandma from Florida? Why wasn't I called?"

"It's not Grandma," I said. "It's an obscene phone caller."

"Oh. We really oughta call Grandma now that we know where the phone is. We haven't talked with her since Christmas."

Finally, I said to my caller, "Look, the timer on the stove is going off because I have been on the phone ten minutes now, my daughter is demonstrating right here in the closet, my son is forcing me to drink down a no. 2 can of orange juice and my husband wants me to call Florida. If it isn't too much trouble, could you call back?"

There was a silence on the other end, then a curt, "Forget it, lady," before the click.

The but-everybody's-got-a-pony syndrome

This phase is sometimes diagnosed as measles. The teen-ager will become hot and feverish (often breaking out in a rash on his or her stomach), will stand on the threshold of hysteria and shout, "But you don't understand. Every kid in school has a three-armed sweater and if I don't have one I might just as well drop out."

This is his need to conform and become acceptable. As a mother, I often wonder what would happen if one day word got around that the class president wore raggy underwear. I can just visualize a morning at our house.

"Mother, where are my raggy underwear?"

"I just polished the piano with them. They're in the dirty clothes hamper."

"You *didn't!* Why do you always have to take my things?"

"I'm sorry. I also threw away three apple cores under your bed, a used nose tissue and a stack of toenail clippings in your bathroom. If you rush, you can save them from the trash can."

"Really, Mother, just because you and Dad don't know anyone personally who wears raggy underwear, you jump to the conclusion there is something wrong with it."

"Who's jumping? Did I say anything when you chopped the legs off those slacks and fringed the bottoms? I did not. Did I say anything when you decided to go without socks? I did not. Did I even complain when you took Daddy's old Army coat, rolled up the sleeves and wore it with a three-foot wool scarf tied around your head? I did not."

"Sure, but now I'll be the only one in school without raggy underwear and I'll feel ridiculous."

"Okay," I said, "I wouldn't want you to grow up to be weird. Why don't we take a good pair of underwear and grub them?"

"You know what you are, Mother, you're g-r-o-o-v-y."

Spurred on by instant popularity, I proceeded to distress all of my daughter's underwear. When she arrived home from school I proudly displayed them.

"See what I've done? You're going to be so 'in' with raggy underwear, we may be under surveillance by the welfare department."

"You didn't," she screamed.

"But I thought it was in," I stammered.

"That was this morning," she sobbed. "Tomorrow, everyone is wearing credit card earrings and skirts with broken zippers. I'll be a c-l-o-d."

"And I'll have the shiniest piano in town."

"A SCARF? Nobody wears a SCARF!"

"Mom, have you seen my scarf?"

2

How to build a teen-ager — if you want to

BIL KEANE

Sometimes I wake my son up in the middle of the night and ask him to smile. Those braces that twinkle in the darkness represent my fur coat, my trip to Monaco, my second car, my college education, my insurance policy (for my old age next week), the operation on my sinus passages.

It seems like only $2000 ago that we sat in the dentist's office and discussed my son's teeth.

"Have you looked in your son's mouth lately?" he asked.

"Actually, no."

"He has a bite problem," he said.

"I find that hard to believe."

"Do you base this on something scientific?"

"I base it on the fact that I go to the grocery store every three hours to keep him fed."

"He has one tooth erupting in the roof of his mouth and if you will note, his molars do not meet."

"You're trying to tell me my son is a werewolf?"

"I am simply trying to tell you if the teeth are not corrected he may suffer some permanent damage to the formation of his teeth."

"What would happen if we ignored it?"

"He could try to develop his personality and buy his way to the prom but . . ."

"I understand. What do you want me to do?"

"I want you to schedule the boy with an orthodontist. He'll take X rays, give him fluoride treatments and set up a long-range plan for his teeth."

My husband reacted with his usual parental concern. "How much is all this going to cost?" he asked.

"A couple of thousand dollars."

"Why couldn't he have had something cheap like bad breath?" he snapped.

"Ask your side of the family," I retorted. "They're the ones with all the crooked teeth. If your grandfather hadn't been so tight with a buck he could have improved on the genes and your son might have straight teeth today."

"It's no use blaming people," he said. "What's done is done. We'll go the orthodontist route."

The orthodontist route, if not a rocky one, was a steady one. At least once every three weeks found me sitting in the waiting room reading the *Bleeding Gums Journal*. After every visit I would have the same conversation with my son.

"When are you going to open your mouth?"

"Never."

"You can't go on day after day clenching your lips together. How are we going to know if your tonsils are bad? And if they are, how are we ever going to get them out? Through your nostrils? You're being ridiculous, you know. Thousands of teen-agers wear braces."

"Name me two."

"Personally, I think they're rather sexy."

"I look like a computer."

"You do not look like a computer. Did I ever tell you what my grandmother told me when I had to wear a bag of garlic around my neck during freshman orientation?"

"Yes."

"Oh, well, anyway one day you'll forget yourself and open your mouth and laugh right out loud and some beautiful girl will say, 'Oh, are those $2000 worth of braces in your mouth? I hardly noticed them at all.' Are you sure I told you the story my grandmother told me when I had to wear a bag of garlic around my neck during freshman orientation?"

"Yes."

This went on nearly two years. Then one afternoon my son and I were standing at the bus stop when I noticed a pert, little brunette ogling him. She smiled shyly at first, showing a dimple in the corner of her mouth. Then she smiled broadly.

Suddenly, all the resentment in me began to build. I thought of all the sacrifices for those lousy braces. The new slipcovers . . . the permanents . . . the colored TV set . . . the support stockings and something in me snapped. I went over to the girl and whispered, "Believe me, darling, my boy is not for you. I know you think that now, seeing that row of straight, white teeth that become straighter by the hour. But just believe me when I say that someday you'll meet some nice boy with a bite problem who will make you a wonderful husband."

Later, my son said to me, "Mom, what did you say to that girl at the bus stop? She didn't even wait for the bus."

"I didn't bring you this far to have you run off with two front teeth that overlap!"

We rode home in silence.

"But, Mom! I can't get glasses!
They make a person look GROSS!"

Call it a mother's intuition. I can always tell when my son loses his glasses. On arriving home from school, he will nod to the dog and rub me playfully on my stomach. Then he will open the dryer and yell, "What's for snack?"

Actually, my son has been wearing glasses for nearly three years. I saw him in them just once. It was in the doctor's office when he was being fitted. For nearly twenty minutes the doctor adjusted the frames with meticulous accuracy, bending the stems to give just the right amount of pressure to the head and nose.

"How does that feel, son?" he asked.

"Swell," was the answer.

"I can adjust them to set a little farther down . . . just a fraction."

"No," said my son, "it's perfect."

They both faced the mirror and with agonizing preciseness the doctor angled the glasses at $\frac{1}{32}$ of a degree to attain just the proper balance. The doctor seemed pleased with himself. "Perfect," he said. "Here is a genuine cowhide case for carrying them."

My son whipped off the glasses, jammed them into his rear pocket and left the glass case (genuine cowhide) lying on the counter.

You would not believe the places we have found my son's glasses. Try.

Inside a boot with a hockey puck and a lost mitten.

In a leftover dish in the refrigerator.

On page 73 of *Catcher in the Rye*.

Tied to the handlebars of his bicycle with a gym shoe string.

In the spin cycle of the washer.

In the glove compartment of the car belonging to his best friend whom he only knows as "Moose."

On top of a soft-drink machine in a service station in northern Michigan.

In the U.S. mail box with a stack of Christmas cards.

Held captive under a fat woman on a bleacher at the city league basketball game.

In a soap dish in the shower of the YMCA.

Looking for what's-his-face's glasses has become as organized as the Ohio State marching band. As the call to alarm sounds, each member of the family goes to his or her appointed area to begin the search with cold, impersonal, detached thoroughness.

The one who needs the glasses (the glassee) sits on a stool in the middle of the kitchen and serves as a central message center in case the glasses are found. (He falls a lot.)

The youngest marches to the bathroom area where he checks under the lid, sifts through the wet towels and personally goes through all the pants pockets in the laundry hamper. "The bathroom is secure," he reports. "Only item found were your keys in the medicine chest."

The oldest has the living-room detail. She leafs through books, magazines, under sofa cushions and the loose dirt around the planters. "Living room negative," she reports. "Only a few popcorn hulls in the large chair. When was the last time we had popcorn?"

My husband has the outside grounds which include the interiors of the car, garage, flower beds and garbage cans. "Nothing out here that a brush fire couldn't cure," he yells.

I get the kitchen area which is a bit more detailed. "Call everybody in," I shout, "the glasses have been found in the breadbox."

Sometimes I am tempted to let the kid grope his way through life, but then I say to myself, "What kind of grandchildren will I get from a boy who squints at a pay phone and says, 'She's tall, but she's pretty groovy, isn't she, Mom?' "

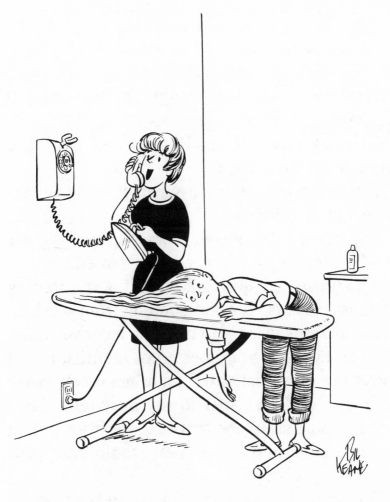

"I was just ironing out some things for Debbie."

I didn't mind when my daughter's hair covered her eyes.

I didn't mind when it cascaded over her shoulders like a cape.

I didn't even complain when it hung longer than her hemline.

But when I discovered it wasn't my daughter at all, but my son, I became alarmed.

The unisexual approach to hair is frightening to most parents. It takes some getting used to. Like, did you ever try to carry on a conversation with an eyeball? For a period of months, it's all I ever saw of my daughter. I'd hear a swish, swish of hair and I'd whisper to my husband, "How would you like to see that emerge from a dark lagoon some night? I bet that would cure your drinking problem!"

"Good morning, dear," I'd say to the mass of hair. "How's every little thing on Eye Island this morning?"

The eye flinched.

"Have some juice?"

The eyeball closed to show annoyance and somehow I felt relief that it indicated life.

"Want your father to drop you off this morning?"

The eyeball went up and we both translated this as acceptance.

"I worry, dear, that all that hair is taking the strength away from your body. You haven't been eating well lately."

In reply, she jerked her head in an affliction that stirred up the long tresses for a second but only until they came to rest again in a straight line that exposed only one eyeball.

"The eye is angry at me and I am sorry," I said. "Incidentally, did you hear the amusing story of the mother who painted her garbage cans orange so the children would think they were eating at Howard Johnson's?"

I should have known better. The eye hardly ever laughs.

The saga of the hair should stop right here, but it doesn't. Very frankly, I got bored with the game. So I said to my daughter one afternoon, "Do you dare to be different? I mean, are you gutsy enough to be a pace setter?"

The eye started to leave the room, then hesitated and finally blinked, showing a flash of interest.

"Have you ever wondered what would happen if you were to cut your hair in a short, feminine style? Imagine, you could sit down without pulling your hair. You could turn your head at the table and not have it fall into the gravy. You could dry your hair in less than three days. Look at it this way. You wouldn't be losing your conformity; you'd be gaining an extra eye."

"I don't know," she hesitated. "That's pretty weird."

"You're a girl," I pressed. "Look like one!"

I never question the forces that move teenagers. I only know that three days later she had her hair cut to her shoulders. As I looked into both her eyes, I felt like I was seeing Halley's comet for the first time.

"You look wonderfully feminine," I squealed. "Believe me, you are going to be so pleased at the reaction of people. They'll look at you and say, 'Now there's my idea of a wholesome American girl!'"

The first outing with the short hair took us to a hamburger emporium. We were standing in line waiting for eight 21-cent hamburgers to go when across from us an elderly couple was taking her in. Their eyes traveled from her short, clean-clipped hair to her bulky sweater, her hip huggers and right on down to her safety shoes with the silver buckles. I nudged her. "You see, already you're causing quite a stir. You know something? You might just bring girls back into style."

The woman spoke first. "If that were my son, I'd cut his hair with a razor strop!"

The man nodded, then looked straight into my daughter's eyes and said, "Why aren't you in the Army?"

All the way home I tried to get the eyeball's attention. One just stared straight ahead and glistened with tears. One remained closed. "Maybe if you enlisted for a few months the hair could grow out," I suggested.

The other eyeball snapped open and looked at me. I wish it hadn't.

3

The hands that hold the car keys rule the world

"If you're teaching Glen to drive, shouldn't the car have
training wheels?"

Dialogue between a mother who was told having a daughter drive would be a blessing and a daughter who up until now believed everything a mother did she did out of love

Mother: I'm not a well woman, Debbie. You know that. After the last baby, fifteen years ago, the doctor said I would experience periods of tension and depression. I am tense and depressed now. What are you doing?

Debbie: Putting the key in the switch.

Mother: DON'T TOUCH A THING IN THIS CAR UNTIL I TELL YOU TO First, I want you to relax. You cannot drive a car when your hands are gripped around the door handle and the whites of the knuckles are showing.

Debbie: You're the one clutching the door handle.

Mother: That's what I said. Just relax and put all the anxieties about driving out of your mind. Forget that behind the wheel of this car you are a potential killer. That you are maneuvering a ton of hard, cold steel which you can wrap around a telephone pole just

54

by closing your eyes to sneeze. Are you relaxed?

Debbie: I think so.

Mother: All right now. Let's go over the check list. Do you have flares in your trunk for when you get a flat tire?

Debbie: Yes.

Mother: Do you have a dime so you can call AAA when the motor stops dead on you?

Debbie: Yes.

Mother: Do you have your license so you can show it to the nice officer when he stops you for violating something?

Debbie: Yes, Mother.

Mother: All right then. Just turn the key and at the same time step on the accelerator.

Debbie: Aren't you going to fasten your seat belt?

Mother: Are you crazy? I may want to leave in a hurry. Let's get on with it. Just gently touch the accelerator.

Debbie: Like this?

Mother: HOLD IT! STOP THE CAR! Let us get one thing straight. The radio has to be off. There is not room in this car for Dionne Warwick, you and me. One of us has to go. You're driving. It can't be you. I'm supervising. It can't be me. Dionne is singing. She is expendable. Now, just relax and push on the accelerator. Any idiot can drive. I do it every day. Just ease along, unwind, hang loose and don't think about the drunk over the hill waiting to slam into you. What are you doing?

Debbie: Stopping the car.

Mother: What for?

Debbie: There's a stop sign.

Mother: Why are you stopping back here? That stop sign is forty feet away, for crying out loud. Pull up. Pull up. Give it a little gas. Go ahead. NO, WAIT! Do you realize you almost sent me sailing through the windshield?

Debbie: I guess I'm not used to the brakes yet. I'm sorry.

Mother: I know. So was Sylvia's daughter. Remember I told you about her? Her MOTHER was teaching her how to drive. She took off so fast she gave her mother a whiplash. I think she's out of traction now. Her daughter is wonderful, though. Never complains when she has to drive her mother to the doctor or adjust her braces. Now then, where were we? It looks all right. Just sneak out and . . . YOU'RE TOO CLOSE TO MY SIDE OF THE ROAD. We're all tensed up. Maybe if we pulled over to the curb here and relaxed a bit. You're doing fine. It's just that you lack experience. Like, when you meet a car you have to remember that anything on his side of the line belongs to him. We can't be greedy, can we? Are you relaxed? Good. Just put your hand out and enter the stream of traffic. Not too fast now.

Debbie: But . . .

Mother: If they want to go over twenty-five miles an hour, let 'em pass. The cemeteries are full of drivers who passed.

Debbie: Do you suppose you could show me how to park?

Mother: To what?

Debbie: To park.

Mother: There's nothing to it. You just go to the shopping center and make a small right angle and there you are. When your tires bump the concrete island, stop.

Debbie: No, I mean parallel park between two other cars. One in front and one in back.

Mother: Where did you hear talk like that? You're driving ten minutes and already you want to get cute with it. It sounds like a wonderful way to get your fenders dented, missy.

Debbie: Our Driver's Ed teacher says that's part of the test.

Mother: So the Driver's Ed teacher is smarter than your mother. Then why isn't he sitting here getting stomach cramps? That's the trouble with teachers today. No guts. I think we're getting tired, Debbie. I have a headache and an acid stomach. Let's head for home. There's a pamphlet I want you to read on "Highway Statistics Compiled on a Labor Day Weekend by the New Jersey Highway Patrol."

Dialogue between a daddy who was instructed to check out the driving ability of his wife's reckless daughter and daddy's little girl

Debbie: You don't mind if I play the radio, do you, Daddy?

Daddy: Ummmmmmmm.

Debbie: Want me to go over the check list?

Daddy: Neh.

Debbie: Could I also dispense with "Mother, may I?" every time I shift gears?

Daddy: Sure.

Debbie: Want to test me on the "Highway Statistics Compiled on a Labor Day Weekend by the New Jersey Highway Patrol?"

Daddy: No. You're doing fine, dear. Wake me when we get home. Szzzzzzzzzzzz.

Dialogue between a father who regards his car as a mistress and a son who is moving in on his territory

Father: Do you know how long it took me to get a car of my own?

Ralph: You were twenty-eight years old.

Father: I was twenty-eight years old, boy, before I sat behind the wheel of my first car. Got my first pair of long trousers that same year. And I apprecia . . . I wish to heavens you'd stop making those noises.

Ralph: What noises?

Father: You sound like the sound track from the Indianapolis 500. Sitting around shifting imaginary gears and making those racing sounds. It makes your mother nervous. Now, first off, before we even start the motor I want to familiarize you with the mechanics of the car. (Lifting hood.)

Ralph: Okay.

Father: Here's the motor . . . this big thing over here. This gizmo is the cooling system and the big square box over there is the battery. Understand so far?

Ralph: You got a real doggie here, Dad. Boy, if it were my car I'd put a spoiler in the front and back to hold the car down, and a four-barreled carburetor . . . maybe even a super charger. Then I'd put slicks on the back wheels for a faster getaway and this old buggy would be out of sight. Incidentally, Dad, you could use some work on your points.

Father: Get in the car, Ralph. And pick that chewing gum wrapper off the floor. Any questions before we get on with the driving?

Ralph: I hope you're not going to get sore or anything. It's not that I'm too proud to drive a heap around but could you take out the dog in the rear window whose eyeballs light up red and green every time you touch the brakes?

Father: Now see here, boy, your mother bought me that for my birthday and I have no intention of taking it out of the car. It would break her heart. And what do you mean with that "heap" crack?

Ralph: My buddy, Steve, has a vet four-speed, tri-power with mag wheels, Fiberglas body and four-wheel disc brakes.

Father: Well, there's a lot of it going around these days. You'll notice over here is the glove compartment. Know your glove compartment. You'll find everything you need here for emergencies. Here's a map of the state, a cloth for wiping moisture off the inside of the windows, a box of nose tissue, a pencil, a pad and . . . *YOUR GLASSES*. That's the third time this month. You know it's immaturity like this that makes me doubt whether or not you are old enough to drive a car. And while I'm about it: What are you going to do about your rusty bicycle?

Ralph: Dad, could we get on with the driving lesson?

Father: Don't use that tone with me, boy. You probably think you got a pigeon sitting next to you. You're not fooling around with the typically square parent. What would you say if I told you I knew what "laying a patch" meant? Huh? I know what I'm dealing with. The insurance companies know what they're doing when they set the highest rates for young boy drivers.

Ralph: In a few months I'll have a car of my own. I've been saving for three years.

Father: How much do you have saved?

Ralph: $27.12.

Father: That dog with the traffic light eyeballs in the rear window cost more than that.

Ralph: All the guys get heaps and fix them up.

Father: We'll see how well you drive this one.

Ralph: Okay, Dad, hang on.

Father: Look, son, this isn't a test run for Platformate. Slow down. You're bruising the tires. And watch out for that car. Defensive driving, boy. That's the name of the game. It's the only way anyone can survive on the highways these days. And don't race the motor. Wait until she shifts into drive by herself.

Ralph: Well, Dad, what do you think?

Father: (Looking ashen) Take me home. I have never seen such an abuse to a car in my life. And slow down. You're driving a lady, boy, and don't you forget it.

Dialogue between a mother and her misunder-stood driver son

Mother: You remembered to open the door for your mother.

Ralph: It's nothing.

Mother: Remember, young man, nothing fancy.

Ralph: Don't worry. You're not nervous and high strung like Dad. Hey, look at the Daytona 500 and behind it the Duster 340.

Mother: Where? Where?

Ralph: Over there. Waiting for the light to change.

Mother: Oh.

Ralph: A fella at school has a new TT 500 and another one a GTX. Dad wouldn't understand any of this. He thinks a goat is an animal with whiskers.

Mother: Isn't he a scream?

Ralph: Mom, do you suppose you could get Dad to take that miserable dog that lights up out of the rear window?

Mother: Of course. I can't imagine where he got such a corny thing in the first place.

Probably something he got with a lube job.

Ralph: You're groovy, Mom.

Mother: It's nothing. Drive.

OUR BOY, THE DRIVER

4

Theories I have blown

"Mo-THER!"

"With emotions ranging from despair to rage, parents look at their sons with matted hair curling over their shoulders and their daughters with ropy skeins over their faces, and wonder why they MUST wear dirty blue jeans, flapping sandals, and assorted bits of clothing usually found in very unthriving thrift shops.

"I have developed a theory about this which may be offensive to mothers and housewives but contains, I believe, a germ of truth. The young like to look dirty because their homes are too neat."

MARYA MANNES, journalist, author, lecturer and political commentator (The Cleveland *Plain Dealer Sunday Magazine,* October 12, 1969)

*"Know what's nice about bein' around home? Everybody can
do their own thing."*

We have an unmarried friend who visits our house about once every three years. Preparation for her visit makes the coronation look like an impulse.

"This place looks like a bus station rest room after a protest march," I announce to the group. "We've got to restore order."

"Why?"

"Because my friend Lydia Spotless is not married and does not understand why we have poker chips in the planter in the hallway. Come to think of it, why do we have poker chips in the planter in the hallway?"

"Because you made us get them out of the knife-and-fork drawer to make room for the keys that don't fit anywhere else and the fourth-class mail."

"Oh. Well I'm going to assign you areas to work. YOU defrost the refrigerator."

"What's defrost, Mom?"

"That's where you turn off the electricity and melt all the ice in the freezer and then turn it on and start all over again."

"Won't the leftovers get ugly if we turn off the electricity?"

"Throw them out."

"You can't throw them out," harped my son. "I was just on the verge of discovering a cure for penicillin."

"Don't be cute. You can clean the stove. I'd do it but I'm a high school graduate."

"How long will it take?"

"Counting superficial burns and skin grafts, you should be finished in two or three days. Oh, and I want one of you to put a pencil beside the phone. I've been in Lydia's house and she has one."

"You're sure doing a lot of fussing for her."

"I know. It's just that her house is decorated in Early Antiseptic. When I visited there last spring, I went into her bathroom and there wasn't one basketball in sight."

"Where does she keep her basketballs?"

"I have no idea."

"She certainly sounds weird."

"Whatever she sounds, we are going all out for her. You all get busy. I am going to take the ironing board down."

"A kitchen without an ironing board? Are you kidding, Mom. It's un-American. It's like Simon without Garfunkel."

"I never told you this before, children, but there are some homes in America where mothers put up the ironing board once a week, do their ironing in a day and take it down again."

"That's easy for you to say," said my daughter. "But where do their kids put their schoolbooks when they come home from school? Or throw their coats? Or put the dog after a bath? Or stack the groceries when they bring them in from the car? Or do their homework? Or eat breakfast? Or shine shoes? Or iron their hair? Or press dirty gym shorts?"

"That ironing board is family," said my son dramatically. "I don't care what Lydia Spotless thinks."

"Okay," I said tiredly. "I'll give in on the ironing board, but get the Punch and Grow tomato plants out of the dining room, the dog collar and the trading stamps out of the bowl of fruit, the Christmas tinsel out of the carpet and the ping-pong paddles off the washer. Oh, and get the tropical fish food out of the spice rack. Lydia would never understand that."

"Older children, particularly, should be allowed to have clothes that are not too different from the standards acceptable to their friends. A boy with brown shoes in a class where blue suede is the standard for that year is being exposed (perhaps unnecessarily) to attack and ridicule. Parents should be aware of what is considered 'cool' and square among children.

"The realm of responsibility in relation to clothes can be stated as follows. We do the selecting; they do the choosing."

DR. HAIM G. GINOTT
(*Between Parent and Child*,
The Macmillan Company, 1965)

"Aw, for pete's sake! Let's switch to SEWN-ONS!"

Teen-agers generally rate their clothes much the same as movies are rated.

"G" clothes appeal to a general audience. This is any apparel that is fake and furry, short and tight and looks like a donation the missions in Bwantanga sent back.

"R" usually applies to items like raincoats and clean tennis shoes. It means they're restricted to boys under sixteen who are accompanied by their parents.

"M" is a rating for boots and clip-on ties. You wear these only after you are married.

"X's are no-nos and include pastel socks, red lipstick, tie shoes, warm hats with bills, and zip-in linings.

The other day in the fitting room, my son slipped into a pair of trousers and asked for my opinion.

"Personally," I said, "I would rate those trousers 'T.' "

"What's a 'T' rating?" he asked, puzzled.

"Terminal. If you ever cough, the entire seat will go."

"They're not tight," he challenged.

"Then how come your face is beginning to bloat?"

"You don't like them because I picked them out," he said.

"That's not true," I said defensively. "I just think there is something wrong when a boy has to unscrew his feet to get his trousers on. Look," I continued, "I am going to give you a choice. Here is what I've selected. You pick out what you want."

"You're kidding."

"Don't judge them just by looking. Try them on."

Later, he emerged from the fitting room.

"Control yourself," I snapped. "You are really too old to cry. What's wrong with them?"

"What's wrong," he blubbered, "I feel like a wind socket."

"Then it is the fullness that bothers you?"

"FULL!" he shouted, "I haven't seen trousers like this since Hans Brinker and his Silver Skates."

"It beats wearing a tourniquet, doesn't it?"

"Mom, can you imagine what would happen if I wore them to school?"

"Let me guess. The band would form on the front lawn and play Lawrence Welk polkas.

The cheerleaders would chant, 'He can sing and he can dance, but he is wearing baggy pants.' Seniors would put 'PANTS IS POWER' stickers on your locker. Under your picture in the yearbook, they would list, Weird Trousers 1, 2, 3, 4. The Varsity Club would give a dance to raise funds to have your pants altered. *Life* magazine would follow you around with a cameraman who snickered a lot."

"You said I had a choice," he said biting his lip. "What's the alternative?"

"Wear your old trousers."

"Boy," he said shaking his head. "It's government like this that brought Adolf Hitler to power."

"Take it or leave it," I said.

"I tell you what," he said, "let's compromise. How about this pair of bell bottoms?"

"If the good Lord had meant for you to wear bell bottoms, he'd have flared your ankles."

"Look," he said, "I can sit down in them, bend, stretch, kneel and carry on a conversation in them."

"But you can't zip them all the way up," I said.

"Nothing's perfect," he sighed.

"Oh well, I look at it this way. If you get cut anywhere on your body, you can't bleed. There's some comfort in that."

"Honest, Dad, it's NOT a masquerade costume!
It's my BEST SUIT!"

"Thou shalt not use threats. Threats weaken a child's self-concept. The psychological effect of threats on a child is bad. But this does not mean that firm limits are bad. Therefore, threats are useless in improving the future behavior of a child."

DR. FITZHUGH DODSON,
(How To Parent, Nash Publishing Co.,
Los Angeles, 1970)

"You're grounded!"

I was raised on threats. I was thirty-five years old before I realized that if I imitated Aunt Hazel one more time my face would not freeze into a mass of warts.

It was also around that time I discovered I could hang my arm out of the car window and the wind wouldn't blow the fingers off. I could cross my eyes and they wouldn't "set permanently." I could kiss a boy and not break out in red heart-shaped blotches to announce what I had been doing to the world.

By the age of ten it became apparent that my mother had an inexhaustible supply of all-occasion intimidations. And I believed every one of them.

"If you don't go to sleep," she threatened, "the tooth fairy Mafia will pull all your teeth and sell them in the black market." Or, "You wet the bed one more time and a rainbow will follow you around for the rest of your life."

The other day I called Mother in desperation. "I need help," I said. "I've used every threat on the kids you ever used on me and I've run out. Do you have anything stronger that you held out on me?"

"Come over," said Mother. "We'll talk about it."

She met me at the door with a small, black notebook. "I never had to use these on you," she said. "You were such a ding-a-ling I could tell you anything and you believed it."

"I guess I was gullible then, wasn't I, Mother?" I giggled.

"I wouldn't have phrased it in quite that way," she said. "This book is a collection of 'I WISH YOU MARRIED' threats. Are you sure you're ready for them?"

"Oh yes," I said. "I feel like a door mat. The kids don't care about me at all. All they need me for is to run and fetch, scour and flush. I'm only a mother. I have no feelings. Cut me and I wouldn't bleed. Only Betty Crocker flour would ooze from the wound. 'Press this, Mom.' 'Don't wait up, Mom.' 'Eat without me, Mom.' 'When is washday, Mom?' 'Where are your car keys, Mom?' 'Happy Mother's Day . . . what's-your-name.' "

"You're ready," interrupted Mother. "These threats are guaranteed to make them feel lousy."

I grabbed the book from Mother's hand and read some of the threats at random.

"You go steady at fifteen and I'll play you a tape of a labor room at the rush hour."

"May you break your leg while dancing on your mother's grave."

"I'm sick of waiting up for you to come home. May you carry your first born eleven months and know what it is to wait."

"I hope your son calls you at Christmas . . . collect."

"So don't get your hair cut. It'll grow into a noose and choke you to death while you sleep."

"Show me a son who talks back and I'll show you a mother taking a bus to the Industrial School to visit him on weekends."

"Just wait till you have children of your own. Never mind why I am smiling. Just wait."

I put the book down. "These are pretty ridiculous, Mother," I said. "I know when I was a youngster I was pretty easily deceived, but kids today are pretty sharp."

"They'll believe," said Mother, nodding her head slowly, her eyes closed. "Incidentally," she said, her eyes snapping open, "that book is valuable to me. I want you to return it as soon as you are finished."

"I will," I said lightly.

"I mean it," said Mother. "If you don't return that book, may you become the oldest woman in North America to become pregnant."

My head jerked up and my eyes flashed wildly, "MOTHER! YOU WOULDN'T!"

"Shh. He's getting PSYCHED UP to mow the lawn."

"When a teenage group gather in someone's home for a committee meeting, a formal or informal party or a casual get-together, one or two parents should be in the house. The host parents have an obligation to the parents of the guests to be nearby and to be in charge. All of this is ordinary social courtesy."

DR. BENJAMIN SPOCK,
(*A Teenager's Guide to Life and Love*, Simon and Schuster, New York, 1970)

"SLUMBER *party?* When does their slumber begin?"

"It's my house," said my husband, "and I don't know why you and I are cooped up here in our bedroom like prisoners."

"Because our teen-agers are giving a party."

"Now I know how parents felt in Germany in World War II when their kids turned them in to the Gestapo for watching 'Hogan's Heroes.' You'd think they were ashamed of us."

"They are," I said. "Now be still and play the game. Do you want to buy Park Avenue or not."

"I don't know why you couldn't handle the group yourself," he sniffed.

"I told you I am going through my post-natal depression period."

"You've been going through that for the last fifteen years. Besides, I wanted to be at Kiwanis tonight. They're showing a movie, *Birth of a Ball Bearing* with no scenes censored."

"It won't hurt you to play Father for one evening."

"How many kids are supposed to come?"

"It's not definite. Anywhere from twelve to three hundred. It depends on how the word has spread."

"That's just wonderful. You know the party. I know about the party. The New York *Times* knows about the party. But does Ben Grauer know?"

"Probably."

"I'm a fool for asking, but what do you feed all those people?"

"We don't. We just back up a truck of soft drinks and open drums of potato chips and pretzels."

"What time is it?"

"Five minutes before eleven," I said.

"I've got five minutes before I put on my baggy sweater and walk through the room looking like Fred MacMurray."

"You'll do fine."

"I feel like a fool," he mumbled. "What do I do if I see someone dancing too close?"

"If they're dancing too close, they're engaged. All the others dance alone."

"Do I look all right?"

"You look fine. Remember now. Under no circumstances are you to smile at your own children or give a clue that you live here. Just amble through and make sure everything is going smoothly. I'll roll the dice for you while you're gone."

He returned in twenty minutes. His shoulders sagged, his mouth was drawn and his eyes haunting and searching.

"Well, how are things going?" I asked.

"Would you believe there is a drummer in our living room who is a King Kong look-alike?"

"Yes. Pay Community Chest $50."

"And do you know where the wood box is on the porch? Well, there's a Volkswagen parked next to it."

"You own two utilities now and one railroad."

"And a wild red-haired kid is talking with Defense Secretary Melvin Laird on our telephone!"

"You just passed 'Go' dear, collect $200."

"It's not enough," he said, cowering in the corner.

5

The family that plays together gets on each other's nerves

"I know the PERFECT spot for our vacation this year!"

My husband looked up from his paper one evening, clicked his fingers and said, "I've got a tremendous idea. Let's take an instant vacation."

"A what?" we asked.

"An instant vacation. One that is spontaneous. No preparation, no planning. Just go. We'll get up tomorrow morning, throw a few clothes in a paper bag and a few goodies in the cooler and take off to Pollution Lake. Would you all like that?"

"We'd love it," they all shouted.

"Good. Then it's settled," he said, snuggling down with his paper.

"Oh, this is going to be exciting," I said. "We've never done anything impulsive before. One of you kids get on the phone and call the vet. Tell him we'll drop the dogs off on our way out of town tomorrow. I'll put a note in my mailbox to stop the mail and one in the milkbox to turn off the milkman for a few days. Oh, and I'd better get hold of my egg man."

"Do you suppose Frank could take my paper route?" said my son. "And maybe take care of the hamster and the tropical fish?"

"I suppose so," I mused. "Call him and when you're finished I have to use the phone to call Elsa and tell her I won't be able to drop those five hundred coat hangers for the Scouts off on Sunday. Maybe on the way out of town I'll drop them off at Fanny Flack's house. Oh, it is fun being impulsive." I grinned.

"Mom, what should I do about my dental appointment?" asked my daughter.

"Call your friend, Carol, and have her call the dentist for you first thing in the morning. Tell her it's important or we'll have to pay for the visit if we don't cancel. Listen, someone get in the car and run out for some mayonnaise for the potato salad. I'll get the cake in the oven while you're all taking baths. And don't forget to get the sleeping bags out of the attic and aired and the cooler off the shelf in the garage."

"We have a turtle collection in it."

"Then get them out."

"Want me to unplug all the electrical stuff?"

"Don't do that until just before we go to bed. Listen, while I am thinking of it, get your father's shirts. On the way out of town, we'll drop them off in the laundry slot. There's nothing worse than beginning a week without any shirts."

"Mom, I was going to the library tomorrow to return my books."

"No problem. We'll drop them off at the library on our way out of town. We have to deposit a check anyway and it's right down from our bank."

"Okay, and what about someone to cut the grass?"

"Oh, for crying out loud," interrupted their father. "How much can the grass grow in forty-eight hours? You are all making a big deal out of this. It's supposed to be spontan . . ."

"And it is a great idea," I said. "I hate calculated things. They never turn out. But an instant vacation. Snap it up with the laundry, kids. While it's drying I'll get out and buy new underwear."

"HOLD IT!" said their father. "I know I'm a fool for asking but what do we need with new underwear?"

"Can you imagine for a minute," I said, "that I would put this family in a car on the highways with raggy underwear? Instant vacation or not, I have my pride. Can't you see having an accident and a patrolman telling the press, 'The ones with the new cars with all the fancy gadgets are always the ones with safety pins in their shorts.' I'd die of humiliation. There are certain moments in a person's life when they should definitely have new underwear like when you get married, graduate, go into the Army or on a vacation. Maybe you want to be known in the ward as the 'Multiple fracture with tacky underpinnings,' but not me. I'll be back in a jiffy. Do you want me to pick up film while I'm out? Sun lotion? A road map?"

"What about the key to the house, Mom?"

"We'll drop it off at Grandma's on the way to the post office. I wrote your sister, dear. You know how she calls the police when she calls and we don't answer. Have I forgotten anything?"

"That is the most incredible question I have ever heard," said my husband.

"Good, then carry on. I'm off to the beauty shop. Luckily Elaine could work me in tonight. You impulsive devil you," I said, tweaking my husband's cheek, "you'll make gypsies of us yet."

For years, my husband and I have advocated separate vacations. But the kids keep finding us.

We have always said if we could just mail ourselves to where we are going, we might arrive in a gayer holiday mood. But it's all the miles in between that makes traveling as giddy as the Nuremberg trials. (We once picked up a hitchhiker who wrote us a check to let him out.)

Although each vacation spot is a new, exciting experience, the trip by car is rather predictable.

First, there is the blessing of the car, followed by Captain Daddy's "Give 'Em Hell" speech.

"All right, gang," he says, resting his foot on the front of the bumper, "you're probably wondering why we're gathered here today. We're about to embark on what can be a wonderful vacation together. That depends on you.

"First, I want to make a few remarks about the car. You'll notice it has a floor in it. That is for your feet. At no time, repeat, no time do I want your feet resting on my shoulders. A good driver is an alert driver and I cannot be at my best with a pair of yesterday's socks in my face.

"Second, we will not play car roulette at any time during the trip. There is nothing more frustrating than for me to look through my rear-view mirror and see bodies hurling through the air like the Flying Wallendas. As your captain, I will make window assignments each morning. If there is any quarrel with these assignments, feel free to file a grievance.

"May I also remind you this car is not a trough. Any candy wrappers, banana peelings, stale bread, apple cores, broken straws, paper cups or breakfast rolls must be wrapped and thrown away or buried. I will not tolerate another fruit-fly assault like last summer.

"Third, transistors must be turned off while you sleep. Also the occupants of the car will not be subjected to more than ninety-nine choruses of "Ninety-nine Bottles of Beer" in a twenty-four-hour period.

"And last, there will be no reading of *Mad* magazine, *Sports Illustrated* or *Mag Wheels Digest* while we are touring breath-taking mountain ranges, historic monuments or indescribable cathedrals. Remember, you are going to have a wonderful time if I have to break every bone in your bodies. We are ready to start our motor. Good show."

Once Captain Daddy's speech is out of the way, we are in for five hundred miles of the Disaster Lady.

The Disaster Lady is our teen-ager daughter who didn't want to make the trip in the first place and who threatens to join a convent the minute the car slows down. Her fatalistic approach to a vacation makes it as much fun as diarrhea.

The car is barely out of the driveway before she lifts her head in a dramatic jerk and whispers, 'Did you hear that? I thought I heard a knock under the hood. Cecily Ainsworth's dad had that same knock under his hood and the car blew up at the end of the driveway."

If she isn't predicting hurricanes as far inland as Indiana, she's telling you an amusing story of a shark that showed up in some freak way at the lake where we plan to stay.

When you are half a day out from home, she will stir restlessly in the back seat and yell, "Mom, did you remember to unplug your coffeepot and your iron? The last time I saw them they were on." Or, "Daddy, did you get a confirmation on the hotel room? I wonder if it's one of those places where you have to bring your own linens? I sure hope someone remembered to take the cat next door."

Occasionally, she will unplug the transistor from her ear and sigh, "Gee, that's too bad."

"What's too bad?" we ask.

"About the weather."

"What about the weather?"

"The extended forecast predicts two solid weeks of rain where we are going. But I don't mind really," she adds.

I'm almost afraid to ask, "Why not?"

"Because I was exposed to German measles thirteen days ago anyway."

In between Captain Daddy and the Disaster Lady, we have Happy Mouth.

Happy Mouth is the eleven-year-old who is one of the best testimonials to Planned Parenthood I can think of. There is something disgusting about a kid who wakes up happy and goes steadily uphill the rest of the day.

"Hey, do you want to hear the poem I read on the last rest-room wall?" he chirps.

"No," says the car in unison.

"It said, 'Violets are blue, roses are red, If you can read this, you're standing on your head.' "

"That's enough."

"There was a phone number underneath it."

"We don't want to hear about it."

"Can I call it when we stop?"

"No."

"Can I plug in the electric back-scratcher I bought at the last souvenir shop?"

"No, you'll run the car battery down."

"Can I take a picture of your teeth?"

"No."

"Anyone want to play Monopoly?"

"No."

"I'll roll up all the windows so the money won't blow around."

"Mom, will you hush him up?"

Happy Mouth may be put down on the average of once every three minutes, but he is undaunted. "Hey, this looks like a neat restaurant," he exclaims.

I grimace. "Are you kidding? This place will have to be cleaned before they can condemn it. Let's move on to something else."

"I want to eat here," shouts Happy Mouth. "There's a real neat dog inside, see him?"

"I should," I said dryly. "He's sitting in a booth."

"Aw c'mon, Mom."

"Okay," I relent, "but let me give you one word of advice. This place is a filthy dump. I bet they haven't had a customer since the septic tank backed up. We'll all be fine if we order something safe like cheese or peanut butter. Remember now. Something safe."

Happy Mouth is the first to order. "I'll have

the roast turkey and dressing." He grins. Then, "May I use your rest room?"

The waitress blows an enormous bubble and pops it. "You walk past the juke box and turn and go through those two big double doors. You walk through the kitchen and out of the back into a gravel parking lot, then walk through that field about an eighth of a mile down the road."

"Isn't that the service station?" I ask.

"Right," she says.

Happy Mouth is absolutely jubilant when he gets back. "You should see the kitchen."

"I don't want to talk about it," I say, picking at my cheese sandwich.

"It's got a stove with big pots on it and a neat fire extinguisher on the wall."

"It's probably a stomach pump," snarls my husband.

"And the dog out there is real neat."

All eyes at the table focus hard on Happy Mouth. He senses our animosity. "Guess what?" he says cheerfully, "I didn't sit on the toilet seat."

Another fun occupant in the car is the Teen-age Grumbler. Nothing, it seems, is as much fun as he anticipated. He came on the trip with a change of underwear and a single word in his vocabulary, "Gross."

The tours are gross, the statues are gross, the motels and the food are gross, the girls are gross and the weather and the towns are gross. You get the feeling if he had been present while the Red Sea was being parted, he'd have whipped a pocket comb out of his shirt, yawned and said, "That's gross."

Efforts to introduce him to scenic phenomena of the world are in vain. "Would you look at that?" gasps his father. "Those faces carved in the side of a mountain are fantastic."

The Grumbler speaks, "They're gross."

"No, they're Roosevelt, Washington, Lincoln and Jefferson," says his father. "Look here, boy, I don't think you have the proper attitude for this trip. Here we have driven 1750 miles to show you a breath-taking view and you slouch in your seat and clean your fingernails with a matchbook cover."

"I saw a breath-taking view already yesterday," he grumbles. "When do we eat?"

"We ate yesterday," snaps his father and drives on.

If you did not know the background of the Grumbler, you would vow he was sired by a Bank Americard, born in a jet and weaned on Wall Street. Throughout the entire trip, he spews out his displeasure. "That swimming pool isn't heated." "Can't we get a motel with a phone in the bathroom?" "You can't get a decent TV picture in this cabin." "That stupid drugstore hadn't even heard of the *Mag Wheels Digest.*" "They only have three kinds of soft drinks at this gas station." "Make him keep his feet on his side of the car." "I've been keeping tab, Dad. This is your 87th wrong turn, your 18th detour and your 467th profane word."

His father turns his head angrily and opens his mouth.

"That's 468th," he says. "That's gross."

Naturally, I have saved the Family Mother of the trip until last. Upon her frail shoulders rests the responsibility of dispensing discipline, maintaining order, keeping track of the gas and oil mileage, reading road maps and of course getting Captain Daddy to make pit stops with some regularity.

"Don't you think we should stop and get a bite to eat?" I ask.

"Why?" answers the captain. "We just got rolling."

"We got rolling at five this morning," I say. "It is now two-thirty in the afternoon and my vision is beginning to blur."

"You exaggerate," he said. "I wanted to make Goose Fork by four. If we stop you'll all want to go to the bathroom, stretch your legs and get out of the car to eat and that will blow another twenty minutes."

"I feel like I am in a getaway car. We are only human. We have a body that requires food and rest. Our muscles must be exercised or they become useless. We have plumbing that must function. We are mortal. We bleed like anyone else."

"NOT ON THOSE NEW SEAT COVERS," he yells over his shoulder.

"That was just an expression," I say. "Frankly, I don't understand you at all. Why don't you get hungry once in a while? Are you sure you aren't pilfering food from somewhere like the fat guy in *The Diary of Anne Frank?*"

"Really," he snorts, "if you are going to make such a big deal about it, look for a place to eat. When you see one, just yell."

"There's a plaaaaaaaaaaaaaace. . . ."

"Where?"

"Back there."

"I can't stop on a dime, you know."

"Not going seventy miles an hour you can't."

"Look," he growled, "you pick out a beanery the size of a flea's navel and expect me to see it and drive at the same time. Besides, it looked like a hole in the wall."

"I thought you didn't see it."

"I could smell the grease when I went by. Believe me, I know when they fry the shrimp and the French fries in the same vat."

"Oh, really."

Two hours later, we are still looking for a place to eat. Family Mother has her head wedged in the no-draft peering into the darkness for a lighted sign. The children are sprawled out on the seats to conserve energy as their stomachs bloat.

Finally, Mother rummages in her handbag. "I'm in luck," I shout. "Here are three breath mints, one for each child. Here is a sticky coughdrop for me and here's a piece of chocolate for Daddy."

Daddy smiles as he devours the square of chocolate. "This should hold us until we get to Goose Fork," he smiles.

"Don't count on it," I say, taking a deep breath. "I just fed you a laxative."

From the back seat came three voices.

"When laxatives are old, they lose their effectiveness," said the Disaster Lady.

"That's neat. I'm going to buy some when we stop and use them as tricks," laughs Happy Mouth.

"You're all gross," snarls the Grumbler.

6

Different schools of thought

"This report card is terrible! I'm ASHAMED of you!" "Your hair is DISGRACEFUL! And those clothes! I hate to admit you're a member of this family!"

"Go, Hank, go! Way to go, boy! THAT'S MY SON!"

"But this IS our homework! We're taping the history of rock music for Humanities Class!"

"We're having a '50s dance, Dad, and we're supposed to dress in freaky getups from 'way back. Can I wear one of your suits?"

"Hi, Dad!"

"My counselor recommended Penn or Purdue, the coach's advice was Michigan, I won a scholarship to Syracuse, my best friend picked Southern Cal, and I like Arizona State. . . . But, I'm going to Ipswich College because that's where my father graduated from."

"My teacher didn't say a THING about my hair. His is longer."

"Why don't you grow up?"

7

Sex is only a three-letter word so how can it be dirty?

"That's not the way we learned it in Sex Ed, Dad. Mrs. Thompson said that . . ."

"There is no need for you to be embarrassed about S-E-X," I told my daughter. "Sit down and I will tell you all I know about it. First, Lassie is a girl. Second, I lied. Sensuous lips do not mean fever blister. Third, I did not conceive you by drinking the blood of an owl and spitting three times at a full moon. Here is the bra and girdle section from the Sears catalogue. If you have any questions, keep them to yourself."

I don't suppose that was too technical, but a friend of mine overdid it. She bought books and charts depicting the reproduction cycles of chickens. Together they studied mating, fertilization and a racy chapter on chromosomes. Her daughter knew more about chickens than any young girl has a right to know.

One day, her mother walked out on the front porch and saw a rooster perched on the porch swing and liked to have had a heart attack.

Anyway, two weeks after my "talk" with my daughter she brought home Leroy.

Leroy was big for his brain. I couldn't look at him without remembering why the dinosaurs disappeared from the earth.

During the two years he was to live with us I can remember only one expression he used. He would come into the house and say, "You look like a drowned rat." (I always looked up and smiled only to discover he was talking to the dog.)

The first time my husband noticed Leroy, he was polishing off a loaf of toast, and a half gallon of milk.

"Who's that?" asked my husband.

"It's Leroy," I answered.

"He's a sex maniac," he said.

"How can you tell?"

I looked the same way the day I stopped thinking of Annette Funicello as a Mousketeer."

"Don't worry about it," I said.

"What do you mean, 'Don't worry about it?' "

"You haven't lost a daughter. You've only gained a disposer with teeth."

We saw a lot of Leroy, which is the greatest understatement since Noah called the weather bureau and got a recording predicting light showers and drizzle.

He arrived in time for breakfast, returning after school, spent the entire evenings, plus weekends, holidays and summers.

They never seemed to do anything together except eat and drink. One day I was passing through the kitchen when Leroy leaned over close to my daughter's ear. I held my breath. This was it. Was he going to nibble on it? Blow into it? Proposition it? I leaned closer, straining to pick up a few words. He spoke, "You got anything to settle my stomach?"

I know enough about sex to know that when bicarbonate enters the room . . . love flies out of the window.

"Hi, Beautiful!"

"What do you think of Wayne?" I asked my husband.

"I think he's a sex maniac," he said in a loud whisper. "He reminds me of a fella I went to high school with. In the yearbook he was voted the Senior Most Likely To."

"To what?" I asked.

"That's the kicker. You were supposed to fill in the blank yourself."

"Oh, good grief. He seems like a nice boy."

"Then why is he pawing our daughter?"

"He's not pawing. They're just holding hands."

"That's all they do. What would happen if they unclenched hands? Would they bleed to death?"

"You make too much out of it. He's an athlete."

"I'll just bet he is."

"I mean a football athlete. Did you know he got a letter this year?"

"So did Hester in *The Scarlet Letter*," he snapped.

"You're being dramatic."

"Why don't you offer them a cold drink to cool them off?"

"I offered them a cold drink and some cookies. They didn't want any."

"We're in trouble."

"We're not in trouble," I said. "Just relax."

I was whistling in the dark. Actually I was quite concerned for the health of both of them. They paled from sitting indoors. Both had lost weight. (At least with Leroy she got a square meal), and they were very awkward getting in and out of coats with their hands clenched together.

"Why don't you kids go to an RX movie or something?" I asked one evening.

They continued to stare into each other's eyes and a faint, "No, thank you" came back.

"Don't either of you have to wash your hair or something?"

Neither twitched a muscle.

"Anyone want to go out on the porch and breathe in and out?"

Silence.

Finally, several months later, my daughter bounded into the house.

"You look different," I said.

"Like how?" she asked.

"I don't know. Like something's missing. I

got it. You're not wearing Wayne this afternoon."

"Oh HIM," she said.

"What happened?"

"He was a drag. All he wanted to do was sit around and talk about himself. Did you know that Wayne has eight red veins in his nose and when he has a cold they swell up?"

She noticed.

"TELEPHONE!" I yelled to my daughter.

"Who is it?" she yelled back.

"It's Bear."

"I got it," she yelled. "Hang up."

"Him again?" snarled my husband.

"Shhh. What's the matter with Bear?"

"He's a sex maniac, that's what he is."

"How can you tell? You've never even seen him."

"That's the point. How come he never comes around to the house? Every hour of every day that phone rings and he's calling. Bear could be a recording for all we know. Besides, can't you just get a picture of a guy named Bear?"

"I visualize Bear as a big, lovable teddy bear who eats out of picnic baskets."

"Funny," he said rustling his paper, "I see him as a big, grizzly with sharp teeth, strong arms and hairy feet."

Whatever Bear was, he was to remain anonymous.

When the phone rang, my daughter would

snatch it and run into a closet, shut the door and whisper into the receiver until we threatened to detonate her.

"What in the world do you find to talk about?" I asked.

"Bear is deep," she said.

"Why doesn't he ever come to the house to see you?"

"He's shy."

"Then you have seen him?"

"Of course, I've seen him."

Bear bothered me . . . or the thought of him did. One night I had a dream that Bear and my daughter were getting married. She was a vision in filmy white as her father escorted her down the aisle. At the end, she was met by a representative of the phone company who joined her hand with a receiver with Bear on the other end.

She was attended by six Princess phones in assorted colors and six black wall phones. During the ceremony, an electronic system played "How Dry I Am."

The reception was even weirder. Daddy and I gave them a chest of dimes and quarters and a phone directory from each of the fifty states. Our daughter left the reception alone. She was going to rendezvous with Bear in a phone booth in Ft. Lauderdale.

I didn't tell anyone about the dream. It was too ridiculous. But the next night I dreamed again. This time my daughter was in tears. "I am getting a divorce from Bear," she sobbed. "I am charging him with harassment. It was terrible. Every time he wanted me to pass the butter, he'd run to the phone and call me up. I nearly went crazy running back and forth to the phone. Of course, there's the child to consider. Do you want to see your grandchild, Mother?"

"Oh yes," I said eagerly, reaching out to snatch the blanket from her. "Then deposit a dime," she said, throwing back the covers to reveal a small pay phone.

I know it was only a dream, but it was upsetting. I had a talk with her. "Look, either Bear materializes before our eyes or we will cut off his phone privileges. This is too ridiculous. You spend more time on a telephone than a storm-door salesman."

Later, my husband mumbled, "Phones are wonderful instruments, but I wouldn't want our daughter to marry one."

I knew then that when Bear called I would hang up.

"Surely you don't think Barney is a sex maniac," I said to my husband.

"And why not?" he asked.

"He's too cheap," I said.

"Just because the boy redeems our old pop bottles and dries out our charcoal and saves it in a bag is no reason to condemn him."

"It's not just that. Haven't you noticed how before every holiday he picks an argument so he won't have to buy our daughter a present?"

"You're imagining things."

"Look," I said, confronting him with a sheaf of papers, "I've kept track."

Palm Sunday: A jealous rage over Elliott Gould that lasted until the day after Easter.

Two weeks before the Prom: Made snide remarks about girls who shave their legs.

Eve of Memorial Day barbecue: Said he had to stay home and wash his hair and she should do the same.

Pre-Birthday fight: Decided he was too immature to go steady and was breaking his mother's heart.

July 3: She laughed when he said he was going to grow a beard and he cut out.

Pre-Labor day weekend: He argued she had a wart on her shoulder and she said it was a mole.

Two days before football tournament: He said if she really cared for him she wouldn't mind taking a bus and transferring twice.

A week before Christmas: He had to study for his draft physical.

Three days before New Year's Eve: He steamed her by suggesting her best girl friend resembled Jim Nabors.

Eve of their first anniversary of going steady: She caught him holding the drinking fountain for a cheerleader.

February 13: Argument over whether or not horned toads bleed through the eyes when they die.

"I repeat. That's insane," snarled my husband. "You take a mere coincidence and turn it into a case for a Philadelphia lawyer. Frankly, I like the way he goes around turning off the garage lights and folding the aluminum foil off the pizza for future use."

At that moment, our daughter came into the room and slammed a book down on the table.

"Barney and I are finished. It's total this time."

"He said the Women's Lib movement was made up of women who looked like Russian pole vaulters and not one of them could make the center fold of *Popular Mechanics*. And I told him to split."

My husband turned to me, "Make something out of that, will you?"

I grabbed the calendar. "Aha. What did I tell you? Tomorrow is Ground Hog's Day and Barney isn't taking any chances."

Bufford had black curly hair, a devilish cleft in his chin and three more teeth than Bert Parks.

He also had the subtlety of a blonde on a bar stool holding an unlighted cigarette.

"Hi, Beautiful," he'd say, slipping his arm around my waist. Then with a double take (that killed vaudeville) he'd say, "Oh, good grief. I am sorry. I thought you were your daughter." The whole bit sounded like a commercial for breakfast cereal, but I always fell for it.

"I like that boy," I told my daughter. "He has charm, breeding, intelligence . . . taste. . . ."

"He also has twelve arms," she said.

"Oh, come now. Any boy who invites his girl friend's mother to a drive-in can't be all bad," I rationalized.

"In separate cars?" she asked incredulously.

She was right, of course. He had conned me into giving him a set of my car keys. ("I hate to bother you when you're relaxing.")

We always ate in the dining room when he

was there. ("Don't fence with me. You did manage the Nixon's dinner parties, didn't you?")

I found myself dieting to see if he would notice. ("Didn't I see you on the February cover of *Seventeen?*)

One day he took me quite off guard when he said, "This is a big house. I figured out how you could make an apartment out of it just by adding a stairway."

"Why would I want to do that?" I asked.

"In case a young married couple was still in school and needed free housing until they both finished."

That evening my husband found me rummaging in a trunk in the attic. "What are you doing?" he asked.

"I'm through messing around," I said. "I've got to bring out the big ammunition on sex education. The bra and girdle section of Sears just isn't doing it."

"You mean?"

"*Poultry Management,*" I said flatly.

"Remember Joey Mackin and Ann Simons from my class?"

"They got MARRIED!"

8

Games teen-agers play

"Listen to this next one, Laurie. It's by The Who."

Hide and don't seek mother

It is upsetting to many parents that their teen-agers introduce them to their friends as encyclopedia salesmen who are just passing through . . . if they introduce them at all.

I have some acquaintances who hover in dark parking lots, enter church separately and crouch in furnace rooms so their teen-agers will not be accused of having parents.

The first time I realized my children were ashamed of me was at a PTA Open House. One of the teachers asked my son, "Is your mother here?" Instinctively, he jammed me into a locker, threw his body in front of it and said, "No, she couldn't come this evening. She's playing pillowcase bingo at the church."

I was indignant. "Why did you say that? Have I ever laughed with cottage cheese in my mouth? Have I ever done my Gale Storm impersonations in front of anyone but family? Have I ever worn my loafers and Girl Scout socks to anywhere but the A&P and back?"

He didn't answer. He just smiled and pretended he was giving me directions to the gym.

If it will make parents feel better, girls in their teens often go through their "Our Gal Sunday" syndrome. It is far more romantic to imagine they were found on the doorstep of two old coal miners and will eventually find happiness with a virile English rock singer than to say, "I was born of Wanda and Louie Fish in a hospital in the suburbs of Cleveland."

Boys of this age go through their Sabu syndrome. They do not want to face up to the fact they were conceived by any other way than without original sin, so they prefer to believe they emerged from a seed in the jungle, fed by werewolves and later adopted by Jon Hall. (Or whoever was Tarzan that year.)

As a parent, I am going through a syndrome myself. It's called Joan of Arc, which means I am sick and tired of being treated like a dog with mouse breath.

I'm sick of scrubbing and washing, running and fetching, scrimping and sewing, hauling and cooking only to have them say four words to me all year: Wait in the car.

Last summer, I drove my daughter and son to the swimming pool. As my daughter and I prepared to emerge from the bathhouse, my daughter stopped.

"Where are you going?"

"Whatya mean where am I going? I am in a bathing suit. Am I dressed for a flu shot?"

"You go first," she commanded.

"Why, aren't they friendly?"

"Mom, no one goes to a swimming pool and sits with their mother."

"It's the bathing suit, isn't it?" I asked. "I should have shortened the sleeves."

"It's not the suit," she sighed.

"The varicose veins then. You're ashamed of my legs."

"The bathrobe covers them," she answered. "What then?"

"It's just that the first thing you always do when you get inside is go in the water."

"I'd feel ridiculous swimming without it," I snapped. "What are you supposed to do at a swimming pool?"

"Other people's mothers don't go in the water."

"I suppose you're referring to Beverly's mother. I personally know she wears a girdle under her bathing suit and has enough foam rubber in her bra to keep eighteen seamen afloat in a tidal wave."

"She's got a neat tan," said my daughter.

"She's the type who tans when she hangs up Christmas tree lights," I snarled. "Besides, I don't trust a woman who sits around the pool reading the *American Journal on Tooth Decay.*"

"Look," she said flatly, "I'm going to sit with some of my friends."

"Wonderful," I said. "When I am ready to go I'll flash my compact mirror into the sun and spit three times into the wading pool."

As I smoothed out my towel, I saw my son stroll by.

"Hi, Junie," I said cheerfully.

"Mom!" he said between clenched teeth. "The guys will see you. And don't call me Junie."

"It's your name, isn't it?"

"Other guys' mothers just say, 'Hey, you.'"

"I'll watch it."

"Boy, I bet they'll think I'm some creep talking to my mother."

"Why don't you tell them I'm a far-sighted movie fan and thought you were Paul Newman."

He made his exit.

It must have been several hours before I felt a shadow over my towel. It was my two teenagers.

"Hey, Mom, we want to get something cold to drink. Where's the money?"

I brought myself up to one elbow, pulled my dark glasses down to the bridge of my nose and scrutinized them coolly, without recognition. "Whatsa matter, kids, lose your mother?" I said crisply and returned to my sun bathing.

That's one for St. Joan.

"Bill and I were just sitting
in the car rapping."

"You were WHAT?"

"Talking."

Twenty questions

Next to having my teeth cleaned without a sedative, my second favorite thing is playing Twenty Questions with my teen-age son at one in the morning. It is like carrying on a conversation with a computer with a dead battery.

"Is that you, Roger?" I shout from the bedroom.

"Who do you think it is?"

"What time is it?"

"What time do you think it is?" he answers.

"Did I hear the clock strike one?"

"What clock?"

"The one in the hallway. Did you have a good time at the dance?"

"Dance?"

"You know, the one you went to. Was it jammed?"

"Who told you it was jammed?"

"No one told me," I shouted. "I'm asking. I suppose you got a pizza afterward?"

"How did you know?"

"I can smell it. A pizza sinks into your pores.

You can smell it until the next shower."

"You want me to take a shower at this time of night?"

"No. I said when you eat a pizza it sinks into your pores, which you can smell until the next shower."

"What's that got to do with the dance being crowded?"

"Nothing," I sighed. "Do you want anything to eat?"

"On top of the pizza?"

"Then you did have pizza. Did you see Marcia?"

"Marcia who?"

"YOUR SISTER, MARCIA."

"Was I supposed to?"

"You mean both of you were at the same dance and you didn't talk to one another?"

"What's to talk about?" he asked.

"Is that the clock dinging again?"

"What clock?"

"The one in the hallway. Did you let the dog out?"

"Why?"

"I thought I heard something scratching."

"Want me to check it?" he queried.

"Would you see if it's Marcia?"

"What would she be doing scratching on the door?"

"Is it the dog then?" I asked.

"Is that something to call your daughter?"

"What are you talking about?" I asked.

"What are you talking about?" he responded.

"Did you hang up your clothes?"

"Can't I do it tomorrow?"

"Do you know how much I spend in cleaning bills because you don't hang up your clothes?"

"How much?"

"Don't be cute. How late is it?"

"How late is what?"

"The hour. I think you are trying to keep the time from me, aren't you?"

"Why would I want to do that?"

"Because it is late," I said.

"Who said it was late?" he asked.

"Didn't I just hear the clock chime?"

"What clock?"

"Roger! Exactly what time is it?"

He was asleep. He had tricked me again. I had had my Twenty Questions and he had responded with his Twenty Questions. I was wide awake.

My husband rolled over restlessly. "Is that you babbling?" he asked.

"Who do you think it is?" I snapped.

"What time is it?" he yawned.

"What time do you think it is?" I retorted.

"I don't really care," he said and drifted off. I shook him by the throat. "Wake up! You've got eighteen more questions to ask or you're out of the game!"

"I don't have TIME to clear off the table! They want us bus boys there by FIVE!"

Parental squares

The saddest teen-ager I ever knew was Stuart Stark, whose parents bridged the generation gap.

I was so sorry for the kid I could have cried. His mom and dad would go around saying things like, "Groovy, wow, uptight and hey, man." They dug their son's records, ate the same breakfast cereal, grew sideburns (not his mother) and protested everything their son protested.

Not only were they a drag to both generations, but they took away Stuart's inalienable rights to play Parental Squares with the rest of the guys.

Parental Squares is a take-off on the old "Can You Top This" game. One boy tells how square his parents are and the next one will try to top him. The first liar doesn't stand a chance. (Not to mention the parents.) It goes like this.

"My dad is so square he still uses words like 'doozy, neato and drip.' "

"That's nothing," interrupts a boy. "We were in a restaurant the other day and my dad called

151

a waitress 'toots.' "

"Listen to this. My dad picked me up at football practice the other night and was wearing knee shorts, dress shoes, white socks and an elastic stocking up to his knee."

"YOUR DAD WEARS SUPP HOSE!"

"Not only that. He has a picture in his billfold of him during the war with his arms around the Andrews Sisters."

"Who are the Andrews Sisters?"

"Who knows? But once I put a fingerprint on it and he almost clobbered me."

"My dad's so square," contributed another voice, "he sleeps in pajamas."

"Mine's so square he hoses down the lawn mower and dries it off so it won't rust each time he uses it."

"Mine saves old anti-freeze from year to year."

"My dad thinks he's a hippie if he doesn't shave on Saturday morning."

"Mine wants me to grow up to be just like the guys in the King Family."

There was a silence before the next round. Poor Stuart just sat there in silence. Then they were off again.

"Do any of your dads wear a belt around their slacks?"

"Are you kidding? I'm surprised my dad gave up wooden buttons on his trousers for zippers.

He's so conservative he didn't buy a pullover sweater until last year."

"Has your dad talked with you about sex yet?"

"It was pitiful."

"I feel sorry for 'em."

"Yeah. My dad got so goofed up he had a sunflower seed making time with a blue jay."

"I know what you mean. My dad was so embarrassed he spelled out N-E-C-K-I-N-G."

"I got the squarest dad of anyone here. He was on the phone the other night and said — are you ready for this? — Okey dokey."

"My dad's squarer than that. The other day I said the meat was 'tough' and he made me apologize to Mom."

"Speaking of moms," said another, "does your mom get shook if you wash your hair before you go to bed?"

"My mom's worse," said a small voice. "She washes her hands every time she pets the dog."

"I don't believe it," they giggled. "You should see my mom. She wears a hairnet when the convertible top is down."

"Oh no. What about mine? Every time my hair grows down to my eyebrows she says the same dumb thing, 'I'm going to buy you a dog license.'"

"Does your mom try to stuff a hot dinner down you when you've just had three hamburgers and a double malted after school?"

"Yeah, and does she always tell you how you can't study, listen to the ball game, talk on the phone and chew gum all at the same time?"

"Look, you guys. My mom is really square. When my gym shoes get a hole in 'em and the sole flaps, she throws 'em away."

"Mine's worse," said a tall boy in the rear. "I gotta win the game with this one. My mom is so square that when I said to her, 'Why don't you let it all hang out and you'll feel better?' she sent me to my room, called Grandma and cried for fifteen minutes."

"Parents sure are weird," said one boy. "Wanta play another round?"

"Neh. Let's go play some ball."

Poor Stuart. He doesn't play ball well either.

"Mother, is it okay if I wear your flowered shift?"

TV keepaway

From September 2 to August 31, the kids have control of the TV set. This means we view the complete football, basketball, baseball and hockey schedules, golf opens, bowling and chess tournaments, tennis matches, boxing bouts, track meets, car, stock and horse racing, ski, skating and soap box competitions.

On September 1 from 9:30 A.M. to 11:15 P.M. I can watch any program I want . . . provided it is not pre-empted by an interview with a toothless hockey player's dentist, an aerial replay of the fannies of the Green Bay Packers' defense, a pregame talk with a dog who has disrupted every Cincinnati Reds' home game since 1937, or a documentary on how left-handed bowling shoes are hand crafted.

It is difficult to single out one sport over another, but if I have to name one in my separation suit, it will undoubtedly be football.

Football is the only televised game I know that can be played over the International Date Line and instantly replayed, stop-action played, and slow-motion played in the East the day before it is played in the first place.

It is the only game I know where if you bring in thirteen channels you can turn the dial from 8 A.M. to 11 P.M. and always find a game that is just starting.

It is the only sport I know that has more bowls than the men's room at Ft. Dix.

The object of TV Keepaway is to drive me crazy. Each viewer drapes himself across the floor, the tables and the sofa. They speak approximately six words a game (none of them to me).

If food is served they will guide it blindly into their mouths, chew and swallow it. If the world were coming to an end, they wouldn't go until after the roundup and final word from Johnny Unitas.

Naturally I have battled TV Keepaway for years. Only last week did I find the answer. Halfway through the game I announced, "How would all of you like for me to serve you dinner here in front of the TV?" No one moved.

"Right on," said one.

"Hey, hey," said another.

"Way to go," said a voice mechanically.

The hands reached out. There was nothing there.

"First," I said setting up the projector and

placing a screen at the far end of the room, "I have some film clips of last week's meal that I know you'll want to see. There's the pot roast being lateraled to Ralphie and the pear and cottage cheese salad that you'll notice is a little offside the plate. We were a little raggy in our passing, but now we know where we made our mistakes."

"Come on, Mom. . . ."

"I have a few notes here on tonight's dinner and a few spot interviews with the butcher, our next-door neighbor, Doris, who made the cheesecake, and of course we'll have a couple of you kids comment on what you can expect from the meal tonight."

"Shhhh," they said, signaling for quiet.

"We're going into tonight's meal with a few injuries," I said, "nothing serious. Both our ends are stuffed from predinner junk like potato chips and dip and cookies, so I may have to play them only for a quarter but . . . Oh, and here's our dog, Lucy, who is going to tell us how she feels about the menu tonight."

"Are you finished?" snapped the kids.

"I have barely begun," I said. "I have my predinner lineup to introduce, an interview from the Claxsons who are scouting us before they have us to dinner at their house next Friday and some vital statistics on each member of the family.

"Now, this little casserole I call, 'Instant Replay.' We had it Saturday, Sunday and here it is again on Monday. Here it is in slow motion. Now stop action. Here's a different camera angle. We'll see how much yardage we can get out of it tonight. One of you may even get it down."

"Can't we eat?" asked one of the boys, rolling over on his side.

"Right after I tell you what I've got lined up for half time. I have 384 black olives that spell out Bombeck on a playing field of pizza, a recording of the Galloping Gourmet sharing with us his biggest thrills in the kitchen and a peek into the second half of the meal, plus Table Scrap résumé, Leftover Scoreboard and Belches from the Stands."

"You win," they said, shuffling to the table. I owe it all to my defense.

9
Teen-age diseases

Virgin feet

The other day my son's guidance counselor asked, "What do you want your boy to be when he grows up?"

"A pedestrian," I said.

I know I'm a fool for hoping. My son has suffered from virgin feet since he was nine months old. Just after he took his first step, he slumped to the floor in a heap and mumbled, "No, na, knee, noo" (Meaning: Is that all there is to feet?).

Since then he has been wheeled about in buggies, strollers and wagons, supported in papoose-back packs, bicycle baskets, grocery carts and car seats, slung over hips and shoulders and transported on sleds, escalators, gocarts and automobiles.

In all that time he has never had his shoes half soled. Never grown a corn. Never worn a hole in his socks. Never gotten wet feet and had his socks fade. Never tripped over a shoe lace.

The other night he stood in front of me impatiently.

"What's the matter," I asked. "Is the Garbage Can Car Pool running late?"

"I am waiting for you to run me over to the school," he said.

"What for?"

"Practice."

"Practice for what?"

"Track. I am running the mile."

"How far is it to school?"

"About a mile."

"How long does it take you to run a mile?"

"About five minutes, forty seconds," he said proudly.

"Then run it. It would take me that long to find my car keys."

"RUN IT! You've got to be kidding. I can't run a mile to school, then run another mile cross country."

"Why not?"

"It's dumb. It's like going on a Boy Scout hike and not riding in a truck."

"Look," I said, "we've got to have a talk about your virgin feet."

"What about them? They look great."

"They should," I snapped. "They're brand new. They've been propped up on sofas and chairs and tables and covered with $20 shoes for the last seventeen years. Now I want you to start using them again."

"For what?"

"For walking. Think of it, boy. This could open up a whole new world if kids started to walk again. Imagine, walk-in movies, walk-in hamburger emporiums, walk-in banks, walk-in sit-ins."

"I can't do it," he whined.

"Of course you can. You simply stand up straight for balance, put your weight alternately on one foot and then the other and extend one foot at a time in front of you."

He stood up slowly and tried it. "It feels awful," he said. "Couldn't I get a motorcycle or a golf cart until I get the hang of it?"

"You'll never get well if you don't try," I said. "Today I want you to walk all the way to school and back."

Later that afternoon, he came limping back from track practice.

"What happened?" I asked.

"I tried walking," he said falling into a chair. "About halfway I got a piece of gravel in my shoe and I leaned down to take it out. A bicycle plowed into me, cut my knee and bruised my leg. I lost my shoe in a ditch and got a sprained ankle when I fell trying to find it. A car stopped to help and got sideswiped. I was lucky to get out alive. No wonder there aren't any old pedestrians. If you ask me, feet will never catch on."

"Have I ever lied to you?" I said, putting my hand on his shoulder.

"Yes. The time you told me the tooth fairy liked to be paid yearly by check to keep her income tax records straight."

"What about the time before that?" I persisted.

Money deficiency

My son did not show signs of a money deficiency until he opened his small fist in the nursery and found it was empty. He leaned over to the kid in the next crib and said, "Hey, bub, you wanta buy an ID bracelet practically new?" He has never been without funds since.

When he was three, he was selling our financial statement to neighbors. When he was six he was underselling the Avon lady. By the time he was nine, he was pulling his teeth and peddling them to the tooth fairy faster than his gums could heal.

One Christmas morning, after he had received $200 worth of toys and baubles, he approached his father and said, "I want to talk about my allowance."

His father smiled, "What about every week if I gave you a shiny dime in return for emptying the garbage, cleaning your room (which is almost the same thing) and clearing the table each night for Mother?"

"You don't understand," he said. "I am not

applying for the Peace Corps. I am talking about a guaranteed weekly salary of $1.50, with fringe benefits, option to negotiate biannually and 6¾ per cent interest on all money borrowed back by you and Mom."

Oh, how I hated to borrow money from that kid. It was like doing business with the Mafia. When a loan had not been repaid he would circulate through our small dinner party, walk up to his father, kiss him on either cheek and place a small, white carnation in his buttonhole and announce in a loud clear voice. "You have until 11 P.M. to repay the $3 you borrowed for pizza last Thursday."

We'd laugh, of course, saying, "Aren't children too much?" but I wished we had enough to pay him everything we owed.

The real crisis came one day in high school. He came home and said, "I have to have another increase in my allowance."

"I've been meaning to have a talk with you," said his father. "Your mother and I have decided we can no longer afford a teen-ager. We are paying you to shine your own shoes, pass English, take a laxative, keep your feet off the coffee table, close your mouth when you eat, stand up straight, be pleasant to your aunt Clara, feed your own hamster, eat a good breakfast, change your shirt and let us use our own phone. The next thing you know you will ask us to pay you to breathe."

"What are you suggesting?" asked our son.

"I am suggesting that you think about a job," said his father.

"Doing what?" he asked.

"That is up to you," said his father. "But if I were you I would begin to take stock of myself. At your age you should be able to contribute something unique to the job market. Think about it . . . perhaps you could do something mechanical."

"Come to think of it," he mused, "I was the only guy at camp who could light a match on his zipper."

"Or maybe something musical," said his father. "A lot of boys today are making a bundle. . . ."

"As a matter of fact, there's a group of us in study hall who can do the Hail Mary in belches." He grinned.

"Or something in an office. Your mother has an orderly mind."

"Yeah. I did have the idea to sleep with all my clothes on to save time in the mornings."

"Or maybe something in law enforcement. Have you thought about that?"

"Sure. Did I tell you I can hang my head out of the car window and make a noise just like a siren? Sometimes three or four cars pull off the highway."

"Perhaps sales is your answer. Maybe you have a hidden talent for selling things."

"Remember the garage sale Mom had and I sold the garage in the first five minutes?"

"Look boy," said his father irritably. "What exactly are your talents to date?"

"I ate twenty-two hot dogs once, packed fifteen boys and a fat cheerleader into a Volkswagen, recited *Hamlet* in pig Latin, did a great impersonation of Warren G. Harding and made a Christmas tree out of x's in typing class."

"That's it?" asked his father, his shoulders slumping.

"What ya expect? I'm only a high school boy."

"Do it again," said his father.

"Do what?"

"Breathe in and out. It isn't worth ten bucks, but everyone has to start somewhere."

"... Plus half of next week's allowance is $4.50, minus the change from Colonel Sanders makes it $3.75 and the $.60 I paid the paper boy brings it to $4.35."

"HE flunked freshman math?"

Convenient Hearing

"Tell it like it is, Mom."

The first time I observed my son with a case of Convenient Hearing, I thought he had been smoking old gym shoes.

I had called him six times to come to dinner. There was no response. Finally, I went directly to his room. He was sitting on the register in a fetal position. The record player was going full blast (Mr. Wonderful and the Electric Pimples). The television set was up to its aerial in decibels. He had a transistor cord in one ear and a telephone receiver in the other. He was teasing a yapping dog with a sock between his toes.

I pulled all the plugs, hung up the phone, silenced the dog and demanded, "Why didn't you answer me when I called?"

He looked up slowly, made a peace sign with his fingers and said, "You know I can't hear you with a war on."

What I had suspected was true. My son heard what he wanted to hear with maddening inconsistency or regard to an individual's sanity.

He tuned on or tuned out when he felt like hearing.

There were many incongruities.

He could not hear the phone ring when he was leaning on it and you were in the shower.

If it was a girl calling for him, he heard it before it even rang.

He could not hear the dog scratch when he wanted in or out.

He could hear his buddies "lay a patch" twenty minutes away from the house.

He could not hear you ask him to take out the trash when your lips touched his ear.

He overheard your discussion of his report card when you talked in a whisper in the northeast corner of the garage.

He could not hear his alarm clock in the morning.

He could hear football plays whispered in a windstorm by a quarterback with a lisp and all of his teeth missing.

My neighbor Maxine was puzzled by our case of Convenient Hearing.

"How do you communicate?" she asked one day over coffee.

"We don't," I said. "My son has only spoken four words to me all year."

"What were they?"

"It was last April. I was separating some eggs

for a cake. As I dumped the yolk from one shell to another, I miscalculated and the egg slid down the counter top, along the cupboard and onto my new kitchen carpet. My son was standing there watching. He looked at me and said, "Way to go, Mom."

"That was it?"

"I was thrilled," I said. "I didn't think he even knew my name."

"I don't see how you can raise him when you don't talk," she sighed.

"There are ways," I said. "There's the old bumper-sticker-with-the-message trick. I hang homemade posters and stickers around his room reading 'HELP THE ECONOMY – TAKE A LEFTOVER TO LUNCH!' or 'STAMP OUT POLLUTION IN YOUR AREA – SEND YOUR GYM SHOES OUT OF STATE.' Of course, there's the ever-popular, 'DON'T LET YOUR MOLARS BE DROPOUTS: SEE YOUR DENTIST AT 1:30 THURSDAY.'"

"Oh good grief," she said, "does it work?"

"Most of the time. Of course, we have to get drastic on occasions and buy time on local rock stations to get through to him. This is how he found out we moved last April."

"I don't see how you have the patience to talk all the time to a boy who only listens at his own convenience."

"The beautiful thing about Convenient Hearing," I said, grinning, "is that it can be contagious. I can catch it too, you know. Like the other day, I was vacuuming the kitchen. The dryer buzzer was going off, the washer was pulsating, my favorite soap opera was on television and the disposer was grinding up chicken bones. My son came out and yelled, 'Hey, Mom, you got $2?' "

I didn't move a muscle.

"Mom, did you hear me?" he shouted. "I need $2. Where's your purse?"

Finally, he unplugged all my appliances and put his face in mine. "Are you deaf?"

I made the sign of the Women's Liberation fist and cross and said, "You know I can't hear you while I'm being liberated."

Prom fat

"No dinner for me. I'm on a DIET!"

Prom Fat is not a disease for all seasons. It manifests itself in teen-age girls two weeks before the prom. Not three, not one, but two weeks.

It is only then that the female species drops her elastic jeans, shinnies out of her bulky sweater, stands in front of the mirror and cries, "What happened?"

Her concern turns to hysteria in the fitting room as she shops for her prom gown. "It's no use," said my daughter, slumping to the floor. "I've looked everywhere and I can't find it."

"Find what?" I asked.

"My waist. It's gone. It was there last fall when I marched with the drill team. I remember. I tucked my blouse in it at that spot and my skirt had a waistband on it."

"It's here somewhere," I said, turning her around slowly. "We just have to find it. Try sucking in."

"I am sucking in," she said.

"This is ridiculous. All we do is look for the narrowest part of your body."

"That's my bust."

"Oh. Well then, bend over and I'll mark the crease."

"It's no use," she said, pulling on the jeans. I have a clear-cut case of Prom Fat. Let's buy the size 7 and I'll diet down to it."

In the two weeks that ensued she was to try the following "local" diets.

CINDY'S MIRACLE DIET

A soft pretzel every three hours (mustard optional)

No water. Repeat. No water.

("What happens when you drink water?" I asked. "You float around the world in eighty days.")

LUCILLE'S EAT LIKE A FLY DIET

Sugared doughnuts (all you can eat)

Jelly buns (all you can eat)

Cakes and cookies

Any leftovers you can pick up.

("Flies exist on this," said Lucille, "and you never saw a fat fly, did you?")

ELSIE'S EAT AT SCHOOL PLAN

Eat in the school cafeteria for five days. This not only eliminates your consumption of lunch at noon, it destroys the taste buds for the other two meals.

IRENE'S DESPERATION DIET PACKET

1 breath mint every three hours
(An 8×10 glossy of Mama Cass pasted on the refrigerator door.)

BARBARA'S BANANA DIET

8 bananas a day
8 glasses of water
(A spare tire hanging from a tree in the back yard to swing from.)

It was two days before the prom. True to her promise to herself, my daughter had shed eight pounds. She looked like Vincent Price, but she had indeed conquered Prom Fat.

On the night of the dance, she ate only her eight bananas and drank eight glasses of water. It worked. The ball gown slid over her hips with ease. The waist had returned. The jeweled belt encircled it like slim fingers.

The next morning I went to her room for the details.

"How did it go?" I asked excitedly.

"It was the most wonderful prom I have ever seen," she said. "There were little jars of soaps and perfumes around the table. There was an attendant who gave you a towel when you washed your hands and when the door opened the music was fabulous."

"What do you mean when the door opened?" I asked cautiously. "You sound like you're describing a rest room."

"I am," she said, "I was there most of the evening. What with the water and all. Besides, I felt faint."

"You mean you spent your entire senior prom in . . . the john?"

"Would it make you feel better," she said, "if I told you I had the smallest waist in the room?"

10

The rise and decline of the parental smarts

"You don't know how many votes this state has in
the Electoral College?
Gosh, Mom, ANYBODY knows that!"

There are several theories on how parents can survive the intelligence of their teen-agers.

1. They can bury them at twelve and dig them up again when they are twenty. (Some feel this is too soon.)

2. They can leave town and bequeath the kids to a recording that says, "Same to you, fella."

3. They can up the cocktail hour to ten-thirty in the morning.

There was a time when the respect and trust my children had for me would have made you sick to your stomach. They believed I could blow on a red traffic light and make it turn green. They believed I told Louis Pasteur, "Keep the refrigerator door closed, dingdong, or the milk will sour." They believed I could knit a broken leg just by blowing a kiss on it. I was riding the crest of the Smarts. Then I reached thirty-five and something happened.

One morning I woke up and didn't know the batting average of Johnny Bench or the formula of the rocket-fuel used in the Apollo 11. I didn't know who invented the folding chair or how to say, "My zipper is stuck," in French.

I overheard my children having a conversation about me one afternoon in the kitchen just after I had written a note for my youngest admitting him to class.

"Bet I know what Mom wrote on your note," smirked my teen-age daughter.

"Bet you don't," he challenged.

"Bet I do," she retaliated. "I'll bet she said you had an upset stomach."

He peeked in the note and then looked astonished.

"That's right," he said. "How did you know?"

"You cluck," she said. "For the last ten years we've had nothing else but upset stomachs."

"How come?" he asked innocently.

"Because," she grimaced, "Mom can't spell diarrhea."

"Just a minute," I said coming into the kitchen, "that is just not true."

"Then how do you spell diarrhea?" asked my son.

"Diarrhea is not on trial here," I said. "You have questioned your mother's intelligence. I know a lot of big words like enzyme, psoriasis and Platformate."

"You're out of it, Mom," said my daughter. "The world is changing. Schools are changing."

"I suppose you think I went to a school where they made license plates," I said sullenly.

"No," she said. "It's not the type of school you went to. It's what you were taught. I'll bet you don't even know what an enrichment program is," she chided.

"Are you serious?" I laughed. "Fred Fronk used it on his lawn last year and he's the only one in the block without crab grass. Of course, I offered to send our dog over. He could tell him a thing or two about enrichment."

"Mom, that's exactly what I am talking about. When you went to school you had only one teacher. We have teams of them. We have a new math . . . in the city experiences . . ."

"I know all about the in the city experiences," I said. "Joan Fontaine had one of those with Joseph Cotten on the late show two nights ago."

"That's another thing," she said. "You had no foundation at all for sex education. I cannot possibly imagine how you and Dad managed on your wedding night."

"Are you insinuating I went to my wedding bed armed only with a white apron, matching headband and recipe for divinity fudge?"

"I am insinuating that you couldn't have been too sophisticated about sex when you insisted they mail your marriage certificate in a plain, brown envelope. I worry about us sometimes, Mom. Lately, we can't even have a meaningful dialogue to initiate the feedback which is so grossly needed."

I walked to the utility room. Kids sure could make you feel rotten. She made me feel as if I wasn't important . . . as if my life was meaningless and drab . . . as if I had mentally deteriorated . . . as if housework did not stimulate me. I grabbed a dryer full of socks and said aloud to myself, "Black with black, green with green, gold with gold, brown with brown, one white, two white, a bluey here, a bluey there and three left over until next week."

I stopped short. Maybe I was out of touch. Last week when someone mentioned anthropologist Margaret Mead, I not only thought she was a foot doctor, I recommended her to three of my friends. And the week before that at a party when someone mentioned Taylor was touring Vietnam, I asked, "Is Burton there with her?"

Was it possible I was not maturing mentally with my teen-age children? Anything was possible with a woman who fed socks two by two into an airtight washer and came out every week with three odd ones left over. I had to try to keep abreast of the times. It wouldn't be easy. I would have to make an effort.

That evening my daughter came into the house and shouted, *"Bonjour, Maman. Comment ça va?"*

"Volkswagen and Maurice Chevalier to you too," I answered, grinning.

"What have you been doing all day?" she asked, opening the refrigerator door.

"I'm reading *Forever Amber* again. This time I'm going to finish it."

"Good," she said. "By the way if you'll promise not to go into convulsions, I'll tell you something funny that happened at school today."

"I promise." I giggled, anticipating a meaningful dialogue and feedback with my teen-ager.

"Well," she smiled, "you remember Debbie Smirkoff? Well, she came to class late today (giggle) and Father Sullivan was subbing for Mrs. Tarkeny (nose snorts and uncontrollable laughter)."

"Oh that is funny," I said.

"That's not the funny part," she said, doubling over and wiping tears of laughter from her eyes. "Father Sullivan looked at Debbie and said (this is too hysterical for words!), he said, 'Well, Debbie, where's Hank?' Everybody broke up!"

I sat there waiting for the punch line.

"Didn't you get it, Mother?"

"Of course I got it," I said. "I'm ready to burst on the inside, but you made me promise not to laugh."

"I don't think you got it at all," she said. "If I have to explain that Hank and Debbie are steadies and wherever there's one, there's the other, then it just isn't funny."

"You think I didn't know that?" I asked defensively.

"I think you ought to get out more. Like Biffy's mother, Barfy. She's on a thousand committees and even keeps a calendar to tell her where to go next."

"Why doesn't she ask me?" I mumbled.

"I mean it, Mother, you're becoming stagnant."

"That's not true," I said. "I am going out this afternoon."

"You're kidding. In that outfit?"

"What's wrong with this outfit?"

"When you bend over I can see your girdle. You should wear pantyhose like everybody else."

"I've tried. I can't seem to get a pair to fit me. The only ones that came close were a pair for women 6 feet 2 inches or over, and then the heel bagged at the back of my knee."

"Then maybe you should take off a few

pounds," she suggested. "I read the other day where women when they reach forty don't burn energy like they did when they were young. Biffy's mother, Barfy, has an exercise program. She says she would no more miss her exercise program than she would miss putting on her eyelashes in the morning."

"I'll jog to the refrigerator from here on," I said.

"Wicky's mother, Wheezie, is a standing," she said, peeling a banana.

"A standing what?"

"She has a standing appointment at the beauty shop. Everyone thinks she looks like Ali McGraw."

"Oh yes. She's the one with the flat stomach who must have carried her babies in a shopping bag for nine months. Listen, I'm leaving now to go to the meeting of the Jolly Girls."

"Is that the group of girls you went to high school with?"

"Yes, why?"

"Honest, Mom, I'd think you could get involved in some meaningful projects. What do you do at these meetings?"

"First, we answer roll call with our favorite dessert. Then we dispense with the medical round-robin . . . who's pregnant, who's menopausal, who's in surgery and who had varicose veins stripped. We talk about having Paul Newman come and speak to us. He never comes, but it gives us something to hang onto. Then we break for chip dip and a sip of sherry."

"What a waste," she said. "How can you turn your back on what is going on in the world today . . . like ecology?"

"I'm doing them a big favor, dear, by not getting involved. Remember? I'm the one with the Astro-turf door mat that died."

"What about politics?"

"They don't need me. I've got four bumper stickers . . . all losers on my Edsel."

"Then what about the liberation of women. Doesn't it bother you that pioneers such as Betty Friedan and Kate Millett are out working on your behalf? What will you say when your grandchildren ask what you contributed to your sex?"

"I'll say, 'Honey, your grandfather gave at the office.' "

"Have you burned your bra?" she persisted.

"I scorched it once on the ironing board."

"Have you ever felt remorse that you bore one and one fourth too many children?"

"Many times."

"Then you should pick up the banner of Women's Rights and carry it to the steps of the Capitol!"

"Could it wait until I empty the garbage on the back porch? If I don't it's going to attack me."

Her shoulders slumped. "For a while I thought we were having a meaningful dialogue and feedback," she said.

"It's me," I said sadly, "I blew it."

"I, Mother, not me," she corrected. "You should watch your grammar."

"I'll be home early," I said. "The church is having a conflab this evening."

"Confab!" she said, her eyes rolling back in her head. "I saw it in the church bulletin."

"Conflab," I insisted. "I saw the women."

As I lugged the garbage off the back porch I couldn't help but hope that my daughter ended the war, adjusted the economy, restored equality, solved pollution, balanced the budget, erased poverty and disease, saved the schools and rendered justice for all before she reached the age of thirty-five.

After that, she won't be able to function as a person, speak correctly, dress herself, laugh, reason, comprehend or spell diarrhea.

"We can teach you French, Spanish, German, Italian. . . . But, I'm sorry, we have no course in Teenagese."

11

Stone age versus rock age

"Sorry, sir, that album has been rated R and cannot be sold to anyone over eighteen."

"Timmy used the car last! Before you turn the key, turn down

. . . the radio."

I have the rather unique distinction of being the only mother in our block to be held captive for a week by two teen-agers and a Woodstock album and to survive.

True, I am not the same woman I was before the ordeal, but they tell me in time I will be able to take walks in the park and pass a wall without pressing my face in the corner.

In the interest of parents everywhere who are concerned with how today's music will affect them, I kept a diary of my seven days of confinement.

It all began on the evening of June 16. My husband was out of town. I was alone with the kids when my face felt feverish, my legs began to ache and my eyes felt as if they were being held in place by thumb tacks. A call to my family physician confirmed my suspicions. "You are sick," he said. "I want you to go to bed and stay there for the next seven days. You have a couple of teen-agers in the house. Let them take care of you." (My doctor also writes humorous one-liners for Henny Youngman and Morey Amsterdam.)

"I am going to bed," I announced to the kids. "I will call you if I need anything."

I might just as well have announced, "I am Jack the Ripper and look at the neat penknife I just got with my new boots." No one missed a beat. One son had his face in the TV set. Another was clicking his fingers in time with a transistor wedged in his ear. My daughter was rigid and glassy-eyed in the middle of two stereo speakers.

Around 11 P.M., the Tower of Babel subsided and I drifted off into a deep sleep.

On the morning of June 17, I woke to the sound of screeching and banging that nearly took the hair off my head. "What is that?" I asked, sitting up. "Anybody? Do you hear me? What is that?"

Finally, a shadow crossed my door and I threw a lamp at it for attention. (I saw Joan Crawford do that once in a movie when Bette Davis was trying to drive her crazy.)

"What's up?" asked my daughter.

"That noise," I yelled, "what is it?"

"Isn't that neat?" she asked. "It's a new stereo tape. Shifting gears with a bad clutch. Wait'll you hear the flip side. It's a muffler dragging in a quiet zone with a police siren in pursuit.

If you don't want to hear that, maybe you'd like to hear the 'Don't Let 'Em Goad Ya into Cambodia Rag?'"

"I have a headache," I said. "Is it possible to turn the volume down a bit?"

"I want you to hear a new group," she said excitedly. "Sweat and His Anti-Perspirants."

"No, really. What about juice and coffee?"

"I don't know them," she pondered. "What label do they record under?"

I turned my face to the window and bit my finger.

Tuesday, June 18. The beat goes on. Fourteen hours of guitar. My head is splitting. I have started to discipline myself by reciting my multiplication tables backward and forward, the alphabet in Greek and the words to "Hut Sut Ralston on the Rillera" and a "Bralla Bralla Suet."

I never realized it before . . . but there are no words spoken around this house. I see people pass the door, lips move and teeth flash, but I never hear a spoken word. Only guitars. Only guitars. Only guitars.

Wednesday, June 19. I awoke in the middle of the night in a cold sweat. Two guitars were fighting over me. I tried to get out of bed, but I couldn't move. One guitar was playing the hysteria of a woman who couldn't get the restroom key from a service station attendant. The other was playing "Happy Days Are Here Again" on a guitar with two strings. No matter who won, I lost. I rolled and tossed and finally sat up in bed screaming.

My daughter rushed to my side and said, "Gosh, Mom, you're all uptight. You need something to soothe you." She flipped on a transistor whose decibels nearly paralyzed me, put it under my pillow and left. I spent the night sitting up straight in bed and listening to amplified belches by the Sickies.

Thursday, June 20. I began to reason if I understood young people's music, maybe it would not set my teeth on edge. I threw my lamp against the door again to summon my son.

"Did you want me, Mom?" he asked.

"Yes, what am I listening to?"

" 'Happy Interlude.' "

"I know that. It's the only lyric in the entire song. But what does it mean?"

"It's the story of a boy whose father walked out on his mother, an unemployed Avon lady. He is raised strictly Establishment, but one day is busted from his job of writing cigarette ads because he is not smoking the sponsor's product. One weekend, he buys a guitar, writes a hit song, meets a girl who is a loser and finds his father who also hates the war. They live together in Canada."

"Who, the father?"

"No, he's with the State Department."

"The girl?"

"No, she commits suicide."

"The mother?"

"No. I told you this is a happy song. He goes to Canada with the guitar. Want me to turn it up so you can hear the words better?"

"No, please. Maybe if you have a glass of water."

"They must be a new group, but if you really wanta hear 'em, I'll check 'em out."

Friday, June 21. I know now I will never get well. That is not their plan. I am a virtual prisoner surrounded by drums, guitars and vocalists who sound like bullfrogs in labor. I can't remember things any more. Like whether or not I am married. Or if I know how to type. Or if my teeth are my own. I caught myself humming, "Go Tell Aunt Rhodie Her Old Gray Goose Is Dead" and then laughing a crazy little laugh. My daughter came into the room today with a new record.

"What happened to the one you played all day yesterday? 'Happy Interlude?' "

" 'HAPPY INTERLUDE!' " she exclaimed. Then she threw back her head and laughed. " 'Happy Interlude' was written yesterday morning, hit the charts by eleven o'clock, was in the top ten by three in the afternoon and as of nine o'clock last night was a Golden Oldie. Really, Mother, you've got to keep current with music or you die."

"The thought did cross my mind," I said.

Saturday, June 22. This is my sixth day of listening to Woodstock and assorted rock groups. My cold seems better. I cannot hear the wheezing in my chest any more. Come to think of it I can't hear the phone, outside traffic, doors slam or the dog bark. My husband returned home today. He came to my room and asked, "How can you stand all that noise?"

I smiled. "What boys? Are they fighting again?"

"Not boys, noise," he reiterated.

"Well, they certainly should pick up their toys before someone breaks their neck over them."

"Are you all right?" he asked, leaning over.

"Fright? I suppose I am. It's this cold. For the last week I haven't even combed my hair. I'll get it," I said, grabbing the phone.

"Get what?" he asked. "The phone didn't ring."

"A lot of people do that," I said. "They just let it ring twice and hang up."

"I don't believe it," he said slowly, his eyes widening. "What have they done to you?"

"Would you face me as you talk?" I asked. "If you comprehend what I am saying, squeeze my hand twice."

He shook his head. "You poor devil. I never knew you were up here in this room with that racket coming from all three bedrooms."

I watched his lips but couldn't make them out. "I'll get it," I said, lifting the phone. He sat there at my bedside with his head in his hands.

Sunday, June 23. Something is wrong. I awoke this morning to a deafening silence. Where is Joan Baez? Arlo Guthrie? The Jefferson Airplane? The drums? The twangs? The "Oh Bebbie's, the yeah yeahs and the uh uhs."

"We are going downstairs today," I read from my husband's lips.

"Why don't you come right out and tell me," I shouted. "I am deaf. I will never hear Lawrence Welk play 'Yellow Bird' again. I will never hear Lester Lanin ask the musical question 'Night and Day.' The hearing. It's gone, isn't it?"

"Nonsense," he said, "I just sent the kids out for the day and pulled the plugs on the stereos. In a few days you'll be back to normal again. After all, you've been through quite an ordeal. Just lie here on the sofa and I'll get the doorbell."

I shrugged. "Who are the doorbells? They couldn't be much if they're not on the charts."

"Turn up the volume! It's the mini-bike solo!"

12

"Why don't you grow up?"

"I'm not CRYING, dear. I was just getting rid of a few of these old things and some dust got into my eye."

"Why don't you grow up?"

If I said it to them once I said it a million times. Is it my imagination or have I spent a liftime shutting refrigerator doors, emptying nose tissue from pants pockets before washing, writing checks for milk, picking up wet towels and finding library books in the clothes hamper?

Mr. Matterling said, "Parenting is loving." (What did he know? He was my old Child Psychology teacher who didn't have any children. He only had twenty-two guppies and two catfish to clean the bowl.) How I wish that for one day I could teach Mr. Matterling's class. How I would like to tell him it's more than loving. More than clean gravel. More than eating the ones you don't like.

Parenting is frustration that you have to see to believe. Would I have ever imagined there would be whole days when I didn't have time to comb my hair? Mornings after a slumber party when I looked like Margaret Mead with a migraine? Could I have ever comprehended that something so simple, so beautiful and so uncomplicated as a child could drive you to shout, "We are a family and you're a part of this family and by God, you're going to spend a Friday night with us having a good time if we have to chain you to the bed!"

And a plaintive voice within me sighed, "Why don't you grow up?"

Parenting is fearful, Mr. Matterling. You don't know how fearful until you sit next to your son on his maiden voyage behind the wheel of your car and hear him say, "My Driver's Ed teacher says I've only got one problem and that's every time I meet a car I pass over the center line."

And you worry. I worried when they stayed home. ("Suppose I get stuck with my son and have to feed him on my Social Security check?") I worried when they were gone. ("If the stuffed animal is missing from her bed, that's it. She's eloped!")

I worried when they talked to me. ("Mary Edith started taking WHAT?") I worried when they didn't talk to me. ("This is your mother and what do you mean Mother who?")

I worried when they dated a lot. ("They're not meditating in the Christian Science reading room until 2 A.M., Ed.") I worried when they didn't date. ("Maybe we should try a sixteenth of an inch padding.")

I worried when their grades were bad. ("He won't be able to get into karate school with those marks.") I worried when their grades were good. ("So swing a little. You wanta spend the rest of your life reading William F. Buckley and basting your acne?")

I worried when they got a job. ("She looks so tired, and besides it could bring back her asthma attacks.") I worried when they didn't get a job. ("Mark my word, he'll take after your brother, Wesley, who didn't get a paper route until he was thirty-three.")

And a tired voice within me persisted, "Why don't you grow up?"

Parenting is pain, Mr. Matterling. And disappointment. The first time I leaned over to kiss my son good night and he turned his back to the wall and said, "See ya." The first time I sat in the pouring rain for four quarters (and a thirty-minute half-time Salute to Railroads) and got chewed out for being the only mother there with an umbrella.

The first time they hit me with, "I'm not going to Grandma's. It's boring." The first time they ignored me on Mother's Day and explained coldly, "It's your fault. You didn't give us our allowance this week."

The first time they left the house and forgot

to say, "Good-bye."

And the anger and the resentment came, Mr. Matterling. You forgot that part. The nights when I Freudianly set the table for two. The days when I felt like a live-in domestic. Days when I felt like sending Betty Friedan a cigar and the kids to my favorite charity. (Or my unfavorite charity.) Days when I beat myself to death with my own inadequacies. What kind of kids am I raising who would let a hamster die from starvation? What kind of kids would snicker during the playing of "The Star-Spangled Banner?" What kind of kids would tell you with a straight face they inherited a world less than perfect? What kind of kids would have a water fight in church . . . WITH HOLY WATER YET!"

"Grow up, won't you?"

And the days of compassion. These were the most agonizing of all. When the tenderness I felt for my children swelled so that I thought I would burst if I didn't cradle them in my arms.

This half child, half adult groping miserably to weigh life's inconsistencies, hypocrisy, instant independence, advice, rules and responsibilities.

The blind date that never showed. The captaincy that went to a best friend. The college reject, the drill team have-nots, the class office also-rans, the honors that went to someone else. And they turned to me for the answer.

And the phone was ringing. I was worming the dog. My husband had to be picked up in ten minutes. There was cake in the oven, a brush salesman at the door and I mumbled some tired chestnut about Abe Lincoln and his thousand failures but how late in life he won the big prize. And then, almost sanctimoniously, I admonished, "That's part of growing up and why don't you?"

And there were joys. Moments of closeness . . . an awkward hug; a look in the semidarkness as you turned off the test pattern as they slept. The pride of seeing them stand up when older people entered the room and saying, "Yes, sir" and "No, ma'am" without your holding a cue card in front of them. The strange, warm feeling of seeing them pick up a baby and seeing a wistfulness in their faces that I have never seen before. And I said to myself . . . softly this time, "Why don't you grow up?"

I shall never forgive Mr. Matterling for not warning me of the times of panic. It's not time yet. It can't be. I'm not finished. I had all the teaching and the discipline and the socks to pick up and the buttons to sew on, and those lousy meal worms to feed the lizard every day . . . there was no time for loving. That's what it's all about, isn't it? Did they ever know I smiled? Did they ever understand my tears? Did I talk too much? Did I say too little? Did I ever look at them and really see them? Do I know them at all? Or was it all a lifetime of "Why don't you grow ups?"

I walk through the house and mechanically shut a refrigerator door that is already shut. I stoop to retrieve a towel that has not fallen to the floor but hangs neatly on the towel rack. From habit, I smooth out a spread that is already free of wrinkles. I answer a phone that has not rung and with a subtlety that fools no one, I hide the cake for dinner in the oven.

And I shout, "WHY DON'T YOU GROW UP!"

And the silence where once had abounded frustration, fear, disappointment, resentment, compassion, joy and love echoes, "I did."

"Didn't Grandma used to be taller?"

THEY ALL PASS TOO QUICKLY!

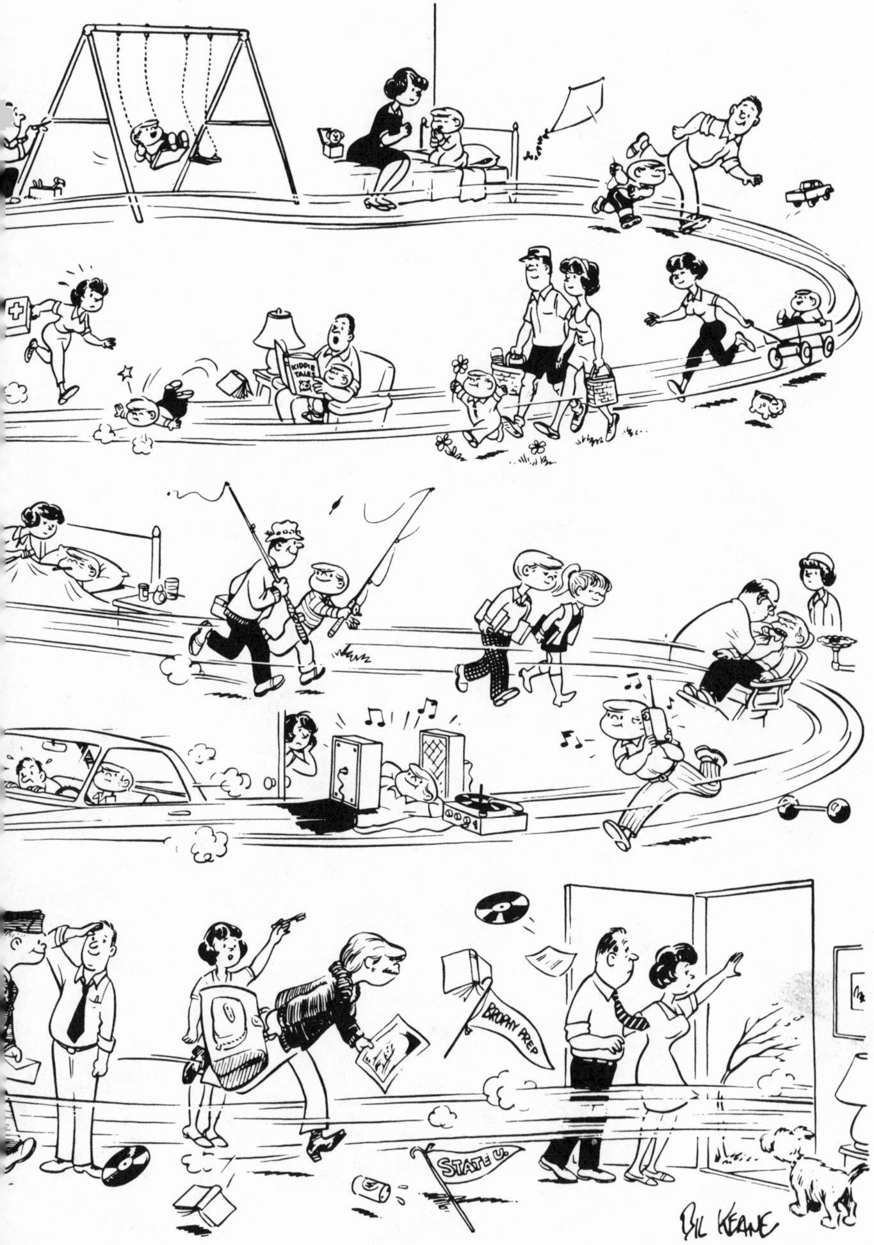